It is so difficult to find the <u>beginning</u>. Or, better: it is difficult to begin at the beginning. And not try to go further back.

—Ludwig Wittgenstein

BEGINNING AT THE BEGINNING

Wittgenstein and Theological Conversation

John K. Downey

Gonzaga University

UNIVERSITY
PRESS OF
AMERICA

LANHAM • NEW YORK • LONDON

Copyright © 1986 by

University Press of America,® Inc.

4720 Boston Way
Lanham, MD 20706

3 Henrietta Street
London WC2E 8LU England

All rights reserved

Printed in the United States of America

ISBN (Perfect): 0-8191-5651-5
ISBN (Cloth): 0-8191-5650-7

All University Press of America books are produced on acid-free
paper which exceeds the minimum standards set by the National
Historical Publications and Records Commission.

For Alexis

TABLE OF CONTENTS

ABBREVIATIONS	ix
PREFACE	xi

Chapter

I. THE SEARCH FOR FOUNDATIONS ... 1

    From Apologetics to Foundations ... 2
    Mapping the Theological Terrain ... 5
    A Sense of Direction ... 15

II. A REVISIONIST FOUNDATION: THE THEOLOGY OF DAVID TRACY ... 27

    The Project: Meaningfulness, Truth, and Correlation ... 27
    The Root of David Tracy's Revisionism: Basic Faith ... 34
    The Expression and Disclosure of Limit Faith ... 40
    A Public Theology ... 49

III. UNDERSTANDING THE WITTGENSTEINIAN PERSPECTIVE ... 61

    On Reading Wittgenstein ... 61
    The Background: Meaning and Method in the Early Years ... 68

IV. LANGUAGE AND METHOD IN THE LATER WITTGENSTEIN ... 87

    Taking a Look ... 89
    Language-Games ... 93
    Foundational Investigations: Conceptual Investigations ... 99
    Language and Method ... 103

V. BEGINNING AT THE BEGINNING: WITTGENSTEIN AND FOUNDATIONAL THEOLOGY ... 117

    Words and Confusion ... 120
    A Captivating Picture ... 127
    Wittgenstein and Foundations ... 135

INDEX ... 153

ABBREVIATIONS FOR WITTGENSTEIN MATERIAL

BB   The Blue and Brown Books

LC   Lectures and Conversations on Aesthetics, Psychology and Religious Belief

Man   Wittgenstein's Nachlass as catalogued by G. H. von Wright

NB   Notebooks 1914-1916

OC   On Certainty

PG   Philosophical Grammar

PI   Philosophical Investigations

PR   Philosophical Remarks

RC   Remarks on Colour

RFM   Remarks on the Foundations of Mathematics

T   Tractatus Logico-Philosophicus

Z   Zettel

PREFACE

Anyone who wishes to become or to survive as a Christian must be committed to understanding, preserving, and interpreting her life and the the Christian tradition. How can one be both modern and Christian? Exploring this question is one of the ways in which theologians have earned their keep. That part of the theological enterprise especially concerned with these questions of method, of how to put one's mind to religion, is called philosophical theology, fundamental theology, or foundational theology. By attending to this area, one avoids building elegant houses of cards.

The following pages address the issues of foundations, of criteria, and of method in theological discourse. Certain philosophers and theologians have emerged as important in this discussion. This study focuses on the revisionist theology of David Tracy and the influential work of the later Wittgenstein. While the importance of Ludwig Wittgenstein in contemporary thought has brought him attention in Religious Studies, this attention is often misplaced, misinformed, or superficial. The present study redresses these errors by focusing a Wittgensteinian eye on one theological example; it may shed light on many.

David Tracy's foundational theology makes an excellent sample case. It is among the best theology done today. It not only synthesizes much of the present thinking, it is also a creative and influential proposal for grounding theology. Tracy prides himself on his integration of modern thought, especially the modern concern with language. His theology strives to be scrupulously public, religiously faithful, and intellectually credible. To refine his revisionist position is worthwhile in itself, though my major concern is to display a new perspective for all theological conversation. It is possible to overlook the role of language in setting criteria for meaning and truth. This oversight is often the result of a fixation on experience and a dedication to a particular a priori view of language. Wittgenstein can provide an antidote to some of the confusion which this bias introduces.

The work of Ludwig Wittgenstein has, of course, been very important on the modern intellectual scene; however, the reaction of philosophical theologians has been tentative. While abundant references to Wittgenstein litter the journals, one finds there also an abundant misuse and misunderstanding of his thought. This is one problem. Another is locating the proper point of contact between Ludwig Wittgenstein and the contemporary theological enterprise. Much of the available material on religion and language is concerned either with the misplaced debate over verification and falsification or with Oxonian analysis. In short, it remains for theology to make the "Wittgensteinian shift." The work presented here is an attempt to outline how and when Wittgenstein might be of use in doing theology.

I would like to acknowledge my gratitude to the many persons with whom I have discussed these pages. Only a few can be mentioned here. Matthew L. Lamb and Thomas B. Ommen have gracefully maintained an interest in my work and have offered many helpful suggestions. Garth L. Hallett was kind enough to read and comment on the central chapters. The personal and professional support of Alexis A. Nelson has been invaluable. I am grateful to my former colleagues in the Program in Religious Studies at the University of Illinois, Champaign-Urbana for help in the initial stages of writing. I would like also to thank the Department of Religious Studies at Gonzaga University—especially Donald B. Sharp and Leonard Doohan—for help in the final stages. For good humor during several revisions of the text I thank Mary Crawford, Lorna Rixman, and Julie Thompson. Good theology is always a communal effort.

CHAPTER ONE
THE SEARCH FOR FOUNDATIONS

Religions have a way of persisting. For Christians it is the story of Jesus which somehow seems to speak to generations whether it is mythologized, demythologized, or critically appropriated. The Christian experience is preserved, studied, challenged, and somehow handed on. These stories, whether they are mythically or conceptually, aesthetically or intellectually elaborated, tell us what it means to be human and what it means to be divine. A good deal of what is handed on is the record of the struggle to formulate a Christian story in a particular cultural, historical, intellectual context. It is never some pure "element" which is passed forward but a version of life, a subtle tapestry woven with the context and texture of the teller and the sources. Theology is reflection on this whole web of traditions and experience in the light of our own contemporary culture and experience. In this way, it is a reflective attempt to assure the survival of religion, to give birth to the "old religion" in a new world. Theology is one way Christianity has of persisting.

Bernard Lonergan has summed up the business of theology by reminding us that "A theology mediates between a cultural matrix and the significance and role of a religion in that matrix."[1] Theology has many facets; there are many levels on which to mediate religion and culture. One group of operations is focused on mediating the past into the present. Another group looks more to the mediation of this tradition into the future. But somewhere between the textual, scriptural, historical concerns of the former and the systematic, dogmatic, pastoral concerns of the latter is located foundational theology. It does not do the actual material mediation in the same way as these other groups but rather sets up the grounds for so doing. Its questions differentiate and delineate the terms and relations which set the frame for theological work. It fixes criteria for properly carrying on. It assesses the credibility of various theological projects. The skeleton of a theology can often be discovered by noting the relationship between religion and culture which it assumes or asserts. In our age of religious, intellectual and cultural tumult, keeping one's balance demands increased consciousness of culture, religion and their relation. It demands special attention to foundational theology.

Theology is an intellectual mediation of religion and culture. This means, among other things, that it seeks to be faithful to the imperatives of the open and inquiring mind and faithful to the Christian tradition. Theology is a discipline of faithfulness. In philosophical theology, the mediation of culture and religion is frequently an appropriation of particular developments in philosophical thinking. The search for foundations in theology is to some extent a search for the philosophical foundations of a theology. The dialogue partners have ranged from middle-platonism to existentialism. The purpose of the present investigation is to make a new tool available to the fundamental theologian: the linguistic turn of the later Wittgenstein. This is offered as a contribution to theological faithfulness. But before we turn to a particular instance of the Wittgenstein-theology dialogue, it may be well to locate the search for foundations within the general spectrum of Christian theology.

From Apologetics to Foundations

Foundational theology is a current heir to what was formerly apologetics.[2] Of course this "new apologetic" is not so concerned with the defense of particular Christian positions as with laying a foundation of certain fundamental principles. Still, it is that branch of theology which has always paid particular attention to the intellectual justification for Christianity, which has always wondered about the proper relationship between religion and its cultural matrix, which today makes its particular task the drawing up of guidelines by which to carry on the theological mediation. The inspiration for apologetics is as old as the Bible itself. Christians are admonished to be ready "to account for the hope that is in you" (I Peter 3:15). This is the natural outgrowth of the universal message of salvation which fired the missionary zeal of the early church and a logical consequence of the doubts and difficulties facing converts to this new minority. Hence the double duty of apologetic as a missionary task and as a necessary personal understanding of the logos in the Christian mythos. The history of Christianity is in some ways a history of those who entered the cultural and philosophical forest of their times with the compass of Christian tradition.

Apologetics is not optional or ephemeral; it is a constant throughout the history of Christianity. Apologetics is given with the double patrimony of the Christian West: Greco-Roman science and culture and a Middle Eastern religious perspective.[3] Through the years Christianity has had to mediate these two strands. It has had to gainsay those who contend that the Christian religious heritage is foolish in light of our scientific and cultural heritage. A good bit of effort has been spent showing that Christianity includes the best elements of Greco-Roman thought. More recent times have seen the meaning of standard terms such as "revelation" and "reason" challenged and changed by a new science and a new history. The realization that religion is always a function of a cultural milieu has made apologetics even more important and its concerns more central to religious practice. Questions of cultural relativism have suggested the possibility of religious, moral and intellectual relativism. As the audience and the culture have changed, the need for apologetic has changed. In the modern period the favored audience for apologetics has become those inside a community of believers. It is not simply a defensive tactic geared to outsiders. The emphasis had been on addressing the pagans of Rome, or the infidels of Islam, or the heretical non-Catholic Christians of the Reformation, or suspicious, Enlightened critics armed with new natural and social sciences and philosophy. But the audience has shifted and the apologist has become the foundational theologian. Fundamental theology is now directed at the believer's search for an understanding of her own faith and culture. Most of today's fundamental theologians write first for themselves and their communities; they seek their own intellectual and cultural roots and insist that true faith calls for self-conscious reflection on the mediation of religion and its matrix.[4] But the task is the same: to preserve the integrity of the Christian message while presenting it as a real option for thoughtful people of the time. Since the task of apologetics is given with the Christian heritage and with the general fact that Christianity exists in varying cultural and intellectual media, there is little surprise over noting the permanence of the issue of the proper relation of religion and culture. Some version of the correlation of these factors is an ongoing part of religion and theology.

The shape of an apologetic depends to some extent on the paradigms offered it by its cultural partner. While the problem of correlation has remained, the name "apologetics" has disappeared as the concerns grouped under its care have been shaped by what Bernard Lonergan calls the shift from a classicist to an empirical culture. The apologetic task has not ended, but it has been transformed.

Classicist culture was a permanent achievement, a picture of the way the world had to be, which supplied norms applicable everywhere and in all cases. Those who were unaware of these norms had to be educated. "Apologetic" was the proper stance of those who knew the outline of this culture and drew their religion within it. They showed the less fortunate--the ignorant--the reasonableness of that eternal truth or extrapolated various fundamental theses from the major premises of scripture and tradition. This culture was marked by its permanence, its reliance on deductive method, and the consequent necessity of its conclusions.

But human consciousness evolves.[5] Modern science and history arose, the Enlightenment struck, and culture came to be characteristically empirical. The world was never the same. It became changing and relative, its particulars were studied by induction, and their relation and behavior was a matter of probability. One might say that the new horizon was characterized by motion. The static world yielded to a dynamic world in process. Modern science and scholarship relied not on discovered or revealed principles, not on logic and deduction alone, but on inductive empirical approaches. One was concerned to understand data and to revise that understanding in light of contrary data. The new culture was scientific in a new way. The certainty of a casual, necessary, and absolutely true science was gone: causality became correlation and conjunction; necessity yielded to talk of what could have been otherwise but happened here and now to be so; instead of _the_ truth one settled for a higher probability.[6] This new culture saw itself not as a once and future norm but rather as a contingent--if useful--matrix of meanings and values held at one point in the universe. The contemplation and extrapolation of fixed values and structures was undermined by the study of particulars. Scientific inquiry began to cast a shadow over its ancestors. The relation of various intellectual disciplines shifted. Philosophy became more than theology's handmaiden and science more than a subset of philosophy. Each began to insure its emancipation and differentiation by responding in its own way to methodological exigencies. Reason demanded and got its autonomy, its identity and differentiations: philosophy rejected the reins of theology as an imposition and later science rejected the methodological restrictions of philosophy.[7] Culture and theology became more a posteriori and empirical and less a priori and dogmatic.

The theological landscape[8] had changed. Eternal truths were replaced by developing doctrines. The ground for apologetic surety was gone. Theology came to be seen as an ongoing development rather than the permanent achievement of a permanent culture. Theologically valid formulae were discovered to be as various as the cultures that spawned them. Clearly, the doctrines of the future were as unknowable as the design of that future. In this environment of changing and competing cultures, religious certainty could not be derived from an alliance with the one permanent culture. Where could a theologian stand? A foundation was needed. It was discovered that stability could be achieved with the lifeline of appropriate method. The new empirical culture was hopelessly secular and pluralist. The new apologetic would have to be equally public and fundamentally methodological.

The contemporary counterpart of apologetics[9]--philosophical theology, fundamental theology, foundational theology--is absorbed with the question of method. In the setting of empiricist culture modern theology began to look, as did the successful sciences, to method. As data and understandings proliferated and became more and more complex, method seemed the only stable platform from which to sort through them. If no culturally conditioned theory was a guarantee, then perhaps proper use of the proper method could be. At least a good method would insure openness to changes in data and understanding. Empirical culture and science set a new tone for the appropriate method, much as Greek science and logic had before it. Theology had to become an open-ended, self-grounding, and a posteriori inquiry. The role of closed, a priori definition must be minimal. Theology must proceed according to criteria for free intellectual inquiry available to the community of scholars. At the very least this means public presentation and justification of one's criteria and procedures. As contemporary science, theology, and philosophy--not to mention the mandates of Vatican Council II--spread the uncertainty of change and the confusion of intellectual, social and religious pluralism, contemporary theologians began to emphasize the priority of formulating one's theological method.[10] What is the proper way to do theology? What are the governing terms and relations? What warrants are acceptable? Theologians must become a methodologically self-conscious and self-correcting community.

4

The precise nature of fundamental theology is an ongoing and unsettled debate. It would be misleading to imply that all agree on the best foundation for theology or even on the elements which must compose[11] it. The problem is a pressing one and the solutions are various. Still, a general notion of fundamental theology has been presented. The following points shape our working perspective: (1) Theology is in some sense a mediation of a cultural matrix and religion. (2) Fundamental theology takes setting guidelines for this correlation as its special function. (3) Historically, foundational theology is descendant from apologetics. This evolution includes a change of emphasis in audience (ad extra to ad intra), struggling with the shifts in cultural paradigms (most generally with the shift from classicist to empiricist culture), and conceiving the task of correlation as an essentially methodological setting of criteria for doing theology. Against this background, a review of the major options for religion-culture mediation will provide a greater sense of just what this theology is and will also serve to bridge these general concerns with the specific concerns of a particular foundational theology.

Mapping the Theological Terrain

There are, of course, various ways of relating religion and culture and various ways of dealing with the twin problems of change and continuity in Christian thought. Recently, two theologians--David Tracy and Matthew Lamb--have developed useful sets of models for understanding the theological landscape. These models are intended as provisional aids, not as procrustean absolutes. They highlight the interrelation of religion and culture which shapes a theology. In addition to providing a helpful insight into agreeable and disagreeable theologies alike, they also indicate the range and structure of contemporary positions. Each set of models, though sharing much, has its own concerns and axis. They do supplement one another and together pose well the problems confronting foundational theology. Lamb's models are dialectical; they stress the differences and discontinuities of the various options. Tracy's models are historical and relational; they stress the ties between theologies. Familiarity with these two sets of models will provide a better sense of the nature and scope of fundamental theology than any definition. A definition is frequently more troublesome, more controversial, and less productive than simply describing the concerns which busy theologians.

Our theological context is pluralist and secularist. There are, de facto, various sets of criteria, differing uses of evidence, and multiple methods. The theologian stands amid a confusing clash of beliefs, values, and faiths. Accompanying and stimulating this pluralism is a secularity which insists upon the autonomy of reason and on the value, even in religious studies, of the new intellectual tools characteristic of modernity. "Masters of suspicion" like Freud, Nietzsche, and Marx have made us aware of the blind spots and bias which can thwart and twist our unrestricted desire to know. Modern intellectual integrity includes not only the will-to-truth (which religion long ago sanctioned and assimilated) but also certain controlling structures for the accurate pursuit of this truth. Just as there is bias, there is an intellectual antidote, an ethical standard for carrying on respectable academic examination and explanation. But does the morality of judgment (i.e., the methods and warrants deemed acceptable) required by the scholarly world conflict with that required by the Christian will-to-believe?[12] Is the mediation of religion and culture the mediation of two moralities? Is religious truth subject to the same standards as any cognitive or value claim? Can the modern Christian be faithful to his secular and scientific commuinity as well as to his religious communtiy? This tension sets the terms that contemporary theology must define and relate. David Tracy has developed models for charting the various options. Using the scholarly-religious dichotomy as a key, Tracy has drawn the resulting theologies into five types. Each type reflects a governing horizon for the doing of theology. Modernity and religion are related in each horizon. Each horizon is structured by a certain image of the theologian operant and the material he sees as his sphere of operation. Models are not concrete theologies, but such generalized ideal types do prove useful in organizing and grasping what is moving forward. These "intelligible, interlocking sets of basic terms and relations"[13] provide a context for understanding actual historical positions. Tracy's models arrange the horizons progressively, showing their genetic relationship and complementarity. Openness to revision is the key notion.

The orthodox model for theology operates from the conviction that the claims of modernity have no "inner-theological relevance."[14] The cognitive and value claims of modern intellectual disciplines have only extrinsic relationship to the actual beliefs which are the material of theology. Other disciplines may be used to provide analogous and systematic understanding (dogmatic theology) or a reasoned defense (apologetics) of the inherited beliefs. However, they cannot and do not affect the actual beliefs in any way. Orthodox theology consists of an explicit believer expressing his traditional beliefs. A sophisticated example of this model is the still influential theology of the First Vatican Council.[15] The orthodox defense against modern criticism is simply a firm commitment to the perennial truths and the perennial formulation of the tradition. By ignoring the cultural shift, the orthodox theologian refuses to have the problem of coming to terms with the cognitive, ethical, and existential claims of our empirical culture. Unfortunately, such a theology has a tendency to make sense only to those believers who share one's own orthodoxy. It offers religion integrity at the price of survival.

Liberal theology insists that the claims and values of the modern secular period do have inner-theological relevance. Modern secularity does influence what the Christian ought to believe. This is not just a serious attention to the criticism of the new philosophy, science and history. The liberal theologian feels a personal moral commitment to the secular faith behind modernity; he is dedicated to the value of free and open inquiry and to autonomous judgment. "The liberal theologian finds himself committed not marginally but fundamentally to the values of the modern experiment."[16] He accepts the challenge of modernity as real and yet remains equally committed to the claims and values of Christianity. Attachment to both the Christian perspective and modern culture creates a theology bent on reconciliation. Examples of this liberal perspective include Blondel, Ritschl, Harnack and above all, Schleiermacher.[17] The intent of liberal theology is simply to claim that a true theology must be the product of the best in modern culture. According to the liberal, theology must rethink the fundamentals of the Christian tradition so that they come into harmony with modernity. Of course, there is the danger that the Christian perspective will become so assimilated to modern culture that its own identity disappears. But whatever the dangers, this liberal commitment to the value and import of the modern vision sets the problematic for all post-orthodox theology.

The remaining three models for theology are variations on this liberal problematic. Neo-orthodoxy, radical theology, and revisionism all accept the task of reconciliation and each in its turn attempts a corrective realization of this essentially liberal project. The neo-orthodox claim that the liberal model is not Christian enough, the radicals claim that the neo-orthodox version of liberalism is not modern enough, and the revisionists attack both neo-orthodoxy and radical theology as dead ends resulting from an imbalanced correlation.

Neo-orthodoxy is an attempt to balance liberal theology's excessive trust in modernity. Working out of the Christian faith experience, men like Barth, Bultmann, Tillich and Niebuhr produced an analysis of the human situation which, because it took the negative elements of human being seriously, issued in a more accurate view of humankind than that assumed by the optimistic liberals.[18] Human nature can offer no guarantee that humankind will progress or even survive. This picture of human experience was also more Christian as it was rooted in the fundamental experience of the non-identity (the radically other and gracious quality) of Christian faith; there is radical evil in man and there is a radically other mystery which can save him from it. The foundation of theology is the "explicit recognition of the unique gift of faith in the Word of God."[19] Although these theologians admitted the modern assertion that faith could be misused (Freud, Marx) they stressed its personal experience as a corrective to modern excesses. The material component of their theology was the experience of a wholly other God. Since this God is beyond the pale of anything modernity could produce or expect, it is beyond the modern critique. The intellect can range freely within the limits of its proper sphere, but it cannot go beyond to question the wholly other or our experience of it. This leads to the danger that there might be no close analysis of the possibility and coherence of religion, theism or Christology. After all, these are expressions of a mystery which is paradoxical by definition. In this model faith is complementary to the philosophy and history of modernity. These secular studies scrutinize a strictly human dimension of humanity well, but require the supplement of a transcendent faith to complete their portrait. The liberal deference to modernity is corrected by an experience of faith which provides the point from which to criticize, improve, and fill out the beliefs of modernity. Neo-orthodoxy solved the liberal problematic by insisting that religion can aid modernity and that Christian faith is neither the foe nor the duplicate of modernity but an ally, a totally non-identical, unique contributor to our modern understanding of human being. This sort of corrective was needed. But does neo-orthodoxy draw limits to reason too early? Religion and modernity are related in the neo-orthodox model, but is it more a juxtaposition than an integration? Is modernity taken seriously where it really counts?

Recent theological history has witnessed the rise of a theological model that is appropriately termed radical. Radical theologians agree with the neo-orthodox that Christian theism is non-identical with modern culture. This realization drove the neo-orthodox to conclude that religious faith could understand and overcome various lacunae in our secular self-understanding. But the radical theologians took this same incongruity of theism and modern culture as an indication of fatal lacunae in theism. The truly modern person must reject that theism. The traditional belief in God is degrading and restraining. For van Buren, Hamilton and Altizer, "A conscience committed to the struggle for human liberation cannot really affirm a radical faith in and dependence upon the God of orthodox or liberal or neo-orthodox Christianity."[26] The wholly other God is dead so that men and women may be liberated to the freedom and autonomy of which Jesus is the model. These theologians are so committed to the value of secularity that they see the theologian's task as a reformulation of the Christian tradition which negates Christianity's unacceptable and crippling theism. This model is a corrective to the neo-orthodox thinkers who, though they had correctly located the dialectical relationship between theism and modernity, incorrectly protected the theistic culprit. The neo-orthodox fenced out modernity too soon. Yet one wonders if the radicals have any boundary at all. Is there really any traditional identity left for a Christianity without God?

The best contemporary theology is done on what Tracy calls the revisionist model. It insists on the full integration of faith and modernity. Revisionism differs from the orthodox model because it denies that any one set of belief formulations is universal and self-evident. It accepts the liberal problem of the intrinsic relation of faith and contemporary culture. Beliefs and their originating faith must stand in constant and true dialogue with culture. Revisionism is not liberalism, for it rejects the naive and uncritical acceptance of modern views and shares the neo-orthodox concern that faith not be swallowed up by modernity. Revisionism is not neo-orthodoxy because it does not exempt faith from critical inquiry. Revisionism is not a radical theology because it does not allow critical inquiry to negate Christian theism. Both the integrity of secular scholarship and the integrity of the believer's faith are to be respected. Yet both are to be open to fundamental revision.

Revisionist theology carries on the liberal ideal of reconciling modernity and Christianity.[21] It is seriously committed to modernity. Various modern academic disciplines do and must have inner-theological relevance. At the same time the perspective is post-liberal or post-modern in that it is a liberalism which is critical of modernity. Furthermore, while it insists that Christianity not be compromised, it also demands that Christianity submit to reconstructive post-modern criticism. Revisionism is critical of an unwary acceptance of modern views: they are to be investigated and if needed, revised. Revisionism accepts the liberal ideal of the reconciliation of the values, cognitive claims, and existential faith of modern consciousness and Christianity. But its methodology is more self-conscious and self-critical. The terms it would relate are a re-interpreted (post-modern) consciousness and a re-interpreted Christianity. Reconciliation will not eclipse mutual illumination, correction and confrontation. The revisionist accepts and presumes the distinct contributions of empirical culture and Christian tradition and sees that by their entering into a mutual critique they can merge into a stronger unity. A secular critique may refine our faith, attention to the sacred may refine our secularity.[22]

Tracy's models display the historical complementarity of the various theological options. There are at root only two models: the orthodox and liberal. All of the other models are really attempts at liberal self-correction. The liberal model arose when the new science, history and philosophy were no longer seen as extrinsic to theology. The orthodox model denied the inner-theological relevance of secular disciplines and and culture, but liberal theology insisted upon their intrinsic relationship to religion. It is this insistence which creates the problem of mediation. But liberalism drifted into a naive trust in modernity which denigrated the religious component of the religion-culture mediation. Neo-orthodox theology arose as an appropriate corrective reaction. It recalled that the liberal project had also intended to respect the element of faith, though in practice it had let it slip away. However, this neo-orthodox corrective took the form of a sheltering of faith from all criticism. The radicals could then claim that the spirit of the liberals was being thwarted by the drawing of arbitrary limits to the dialogue with secularity. They called for the unfettered normativity of the secular <u>Geist</u>, whatever be the consequences for so-called traditional religion. Finally, the revisionist model notes that the extremism of both the radicals and the neo-orthodox ended all real mediation and dialogue. Revisionism attempts to recover the liberal program by maintaining a dialogue between the neo-orthodox emphasis on faith and the radical emphasis on secularity.

Liberalism sets the contemporary theological problematic, and revisionism's version of liberalism dictates the specific terms and relations which fix the fundamental theological heuristic. Some form of this general heuristic for a useful theology is presumed in much of the current literature and certainly in these pages. But there is a further nuance to the contemporary discussion. Theology should be public and intellectually sophisticated attention to both religion and culture. Yet, the philosophical tools available for this task are various and diverse. David Tracy favors the use of phenomenology and metaphysics. It should be pointed out that there are those who doubt that these philosophical partners can be helpful. Is reliance on the privileged representation of an epistemology or the privileged structures of a metaphysics fruitful? It may be that the search for such foundations brings more heat than light to the theological enterprise. Is there an alternative?

In order to surface this question and to confirm our sense of the business of theology, it may be helpful to tour the theological grounds again by a slightly different route. Tracy's models accent the genetic and complementary relationship of each succeeding model. With this historical perspective in mind, it will now be instructive to emphasize the dialectic relationship (i.e., the opposition and exclusivity) between the models.

Matthew L. Lamb has developed a series of models which highlight the opposition, assimilation, or mixture characteristic of various theological mediations.[23] Focusing on _fides_ and _ratio_ as representative terms in a discussion of religion and its cultural matrix, Lamb notes the tension of their relationship and the various ways of relaxing it. He concentrates not on why one model gave rise to the next but on how each model represents a totally different sort of relationship between foundational theology's axial terms. Each of these models reflects a specific location of the norms for doing theology. This concern surfaces very clearly the criteriological problem before the theologian. Lamb is concerned with whether a theoretical resolution of the religion-culture tension is adequate. He raises an additional issue in the search for foundations.

In paleomorphic theologies the mediation of faith and culture is in terms of an older (paleo) cultural form (morphic). This is a refusal to admit that cultural change calls for theological change: a formerly contemporary theology is pressed to serve in a new and very different cultural context. A theology drawn up within a classical cultural matrix is preserved in the midst of our empirical cultural matrix. Norms for mediation remain "external and necessary, not in the flux of the universe of existence."[24] This refusal to account for new empirical culture creates an anachronistic theology which clashes with the rest of the believer's empirical world and which is often unaware that it, itself, is a version of a past culture. The theological manuals still in force today and certainly dominant in Catholic theology between Vatican I and Vatican II are obvious examples.[25] Paleomorphic theology unreflectively identifies faith with culture and culture with the classicist perspective. The identity of faith is submerged by an identification of faith with a past version of culture and reason.

As paleomorphic theologies identify reason and culture with past cultures, neomorphic theologies identify them with contemporary cultural strands. Metaphysics is suspect and the problem of historicity is prominent. More to the point, the religious tradition is extrinsic to the determinations of modern culture which provide the real norms for theologizing. These theologies (e.g., "death of God," liberal) are not all that critical of the contemporary culture they embrace and at the same time they ignore or transpose elements of religious faith that conflict with their version of the prevailing Zeitgeist. Once again faith loses its identity in the smothering priority of cultural norms. The error of paleomorphic and neomorphic theologies is the same: they too closely identify faith with a particular culture. Though they differ on which culture they take as normative, both find their norms for doing theology wholly in culture. In this situation there is little hope for a transcultural critique and so theology becomes merely a battle of cultures.

Fideomorphic theology is a protest against any identification of faith with culture. Such theologies claim that faith needs no philosophical or critical-historical mediation; it is quite capable of presenting itself. The norm for theology is outside of all cultural mediations: it is God as He reveals Himself. "Normativity, then, is radically gift and grace in a non-identical relation to human experience."[26] It is not unusual for fideomorphic thought to be coupled with fideism and to stress prayer and sacrament or obedience to the Word of God.[27] Examples of fideomorphism are the "Nein" of Karl Barth, von Balthasar's aesthetic theology and the recent Hartford Appeal.[28] This type of theology advocates a confrontationalist relation to culture. But willful innocence of the cultural aspects of religion often allows fideomorphic theology to drift into paleomorphism, i.e., to simply repeat the past relation of faith and culture underlying the Bible and the Fathers. Fideomorphic theologies want to help religion hold on to its own identity and they want to do so by stressing its non-identification with reason and culture. Christian faith is to be isolated from various cultural contaminations. But will denial of contagion end it? The danger in denying the role of culture and reason in theology is that one will then be unwittingly controlled by their inevitable presence. This naivete about the full extent of one's theological pre-suppositions is not beneficial in foundational theology.

A criticomorphic theology is one which combines neo-morphic dedication to modern culture with fideomorphic dedication to the preservation of the truth of faith. It notes the limitations of both the total identification and the total non-identification of faith with a culture. While theological mediation must not identify religion with culture, it must recognize that they are not totally independent. The goal is a "unity of identity and non-identity," i.e., a bringing together of the common elements of each and a simultaneous preserving of their unique, complementary and even contradictory elements. Lamb calls these theologies "critico" because they insist on the use of critical-historical methods in the probing of Christian sources and because, at the same time, they are critical of contemporary culture. <u>Fides</u> and <u>Ratio</u>, religion and its cultural matrix, are both important and yet each must submit to appropriate criticism. Norms for theology are not wholly in the cultural matrix nor are they exclusively religious: they are generated in a mutual interaction.[29] This mutually critical relation of theology's terms is characteristic of the best contemporary theology. It may take one of two forms; it may be strictly criticomorphic or it may be further differentiated into a politicomorphic theology.

In criticomorphic theology proper, the characteristic critical correlation is theoretic. These theologies are very concerned with the theoretical issues facing modern theology and so seek to mediate by developing a unified theoretical, philosophical understanding. Typically, the unity which grounds this theology is founded in the elaboration of an ontology which can do justice "to both the socio-historical and the existential demands of Christian faith and practice."[30] Notable among criticomorphic theologians are Bultmann, Rahner and Tracy. Each insists on the integration of critical-historical method and faith, each is critical of his cultural matrix and each develops a correlation which is founded on an ontology or metaphysics.[31] At the same time, each insists that this philosophical mediation safeguard the non-identity of faith by positing a crucial role for, respectively, faith-decision, openness to mystery, or faith that existence is worthwhile.[32] Criticomorphic theology is interested in taking the new historical sciences seriously and in justifying their theological import in a unifying ontology or metaphysic. This strictly theoretical mediation of cultural norms and Christian tradition distinguishes criticomorphic theology from politicomorphic.[33]

Lamb's final model is a variation developed within and moving beyond the criticomorphic problematic. The criticomorphic emphasis on the problem of historicity leads it to focus on the mediation of the past into the present. Politicomorphic theology accepts the issue of reciprocal critical mediation from criticomorphic theology; it presumes the advances of criticomorphic discovery of the importance of decision and conversion and the need for an integration of historical science and religious tradition. And yet politicomorphic theology offers a very different mediation of culture and religion. Its concern is with the mediation of the present into the future. This heuristic for the theological task is indebted to so-called critical theory and to the use of this view in the recent work of J.B. Metz.[34] For him, critical correlation must take place not in theory but in a praxis. Theory can never ground itself but rather is grounded ultimately in praxis. Praxis is the goal and foundation of theory.[35] Without getting into a technical discussion of the nature of praxis, one can simply note that it is a call for attention to the non-theoretical basis of theory and the feedback relationship between practice and theory.[36] In this process, "action and its consequences dictate changes in theory and theory dictates actions."[37] This is a call for a new Enlightenment, one in which value-centered human action will not be subordinated either to the concerns of mere theory or to the concerns of mere technique. The end result is the rise of a socio-critical consciousness which can shape and relate science, politics and religion.[38]

Politicomorphic thinkers (Metz, Lamb himself, Lonergan) are convinced that, in the context of our overwhelming pluralism and relativity, no theory can accomplish the mediation of Christianity. Theologians need more than a theoretical integration of historical and scientific method into a theology. Such a criticomorphic solution is merely a theoretical integration of theories and as such cannot escape relativism or claim to be self-grounding. Theories simply add to the dissonance by bringing determinative but often uncritically mediated socio-political baggage. A certain sort of doing, a praxis, a method is the foundation which sets the terms and carries mediation forward.[39]

For Lamb, the theological encounter of religion and culture may take one of five forms: paleomorphic, neomorphic, fideomorphic, criticomorphic or politicomorphic. These various attempts to relate religion and culture differ in how they modulate the relationship. Certain mediations are judged more adequate than others. The first two forms share a common refusal to distinguish religion and culture and a consequent tendency to sacrifice the particular identity of religion to cultural assimilation. Theological norms are dictated by culture. Fideomorphic theology replaces this assimilation with confrontation. Fideomorphic thinking differs in its self-conscious attempt to move away from the naiveté of paleomorphic and neomorphic mediations. Yet it divides religion and culture in such a way that it becomes a sort of a-cultural religious positivism. Each of these first three options is culturally naive; each refuses to see that culture is inextricably bound up with religion and so fails to be critical of the culture which it actively embraces or of the cultural dimension present willy-nilly to religious life. Criticomorphic and politicomorphic mediations seek to retain and respect--and yet to unify--both the cultural component and the uniquely religious component. They strive for what Lamb calls a "unity of identity and non-identity," a unity in which religion can be identified but not identical with culture, a unity in which it remains distinctly itself, a unity in difference. This more accurate mediation can be either criticomorphic or politicomorphic. These two strains are themselves differentiated according to how they would achieve this mediation. Criticomorphic theologies insist on theoretical mediations such as philosophies of historicity or (as in Tracy) a phenomenology and a metaphysics.[40] Politicomorphic mediation is methodological and rooted in praxis. Not until criticomorphism is history taken seriously. Not until politicomorphisim is praxis taken seriously. The details of Lamb's own politicomorphism are a matter for another occasion. His work certainly illustrates the grave doubts among some theologians and philosophers as to the ability of a theory to resolve the search for foundations.

The models of David Tracy and Matthew Lamb have provided a useful occasion for noting some common features of the contemporary theological scene. The differences between these two sets of models may also add to our theological orientation.

Tracy's models vary somewhat from those of Lamb. Predictably where they differ is on the nature of the later models. This is natural since each takes a different point as his pivot. The exact nature of a dialogical theology is the crucial and determinitive point of each typology. Of course, both agree in their concern with method. But a major difference surfaces between the views of Lamb and Tracy on the meaning of method: the former stresses praxis, the latter theoretical revision. Take for example the matter of Karl Rahner or Rudolf Bultmann. Both are criticized by Tracy and Lamb as offering less adequate approaches to doing theology in the modern context. Although their work is very fruitful, it is not adequate to address questions of revisionism or the theory-praxis relationship. Lamb claims to move beyond their work in his politicomorphism, Tracy in his revisionism. Interestingly, Lamb places Rahner and Bultmann in the same category with Tracy.[41] Tracy, of course, claims to have left these two supposedly neo-orthodox thinkers behind him. This may be true in terms of the revisionist issue. Lamb admires Tracy's work, but he finds there an inadequate theory-praxis correlation. Tracy falls into criticomorphism because he turns to theory not praxis for the final mediation. Since he is not politicomorphic, the only model with which he is reasonably compatible is the criticomorphic. Lamb does not distinguish between various types of criticomorphism because no matter what sort of latitude reason and religion are given, the whole project remains narrowly theoretical. From Tracy's perspective, various theological projects are neo-orthodox or revisionist depending on whether they are willing to revise traditional theological understandings. This, of course, is exactly why Lamb sees Tracy's approach as incomplete: he stresses the revision of understanding and not the revising praxis in which it is grounded. Since Lamb ignores the issue of revision, one conjectures that his theology is in danger of being less than adequate on Tracy's scale. Tracy did label the political and liberation theology with which Lamb is sympathetic, neo-orthodox.[42] It seemed the only place to locate an attempt at real mediation that was not essentially revisionist. But of course Tracy and Lamb, while both concerned with the history and future of theology, do draft models to stress their own approach to the problem of foundations. Each looks to a different axis. They construct models either to stress the need for a revisionist attitude or to stress the need for attention to the theory-praxis relationship. These two sets of models are similar enough and different enough to be genuinely complementary. Each set of models is fruitful and adequate--up to a point. Lamb and Tracy agree that the best model for theology is that of an open and self-conscious dialogue. They differ as to the value of theory in this dialogue.

A Sense of Direction

What do we learn from these two pictures of fundamental theology? If one prescinds from the varying foci and interests behind each typology, a certain consensus about the search for foundations does emerge. The theological options can be organized according to the general schema they offer for the relation of religion to its cultural matrix. David Tracy criticizes the non-revisionist models according to their perspective on revision. Matthew Lamb criticizes the non-politicomorphic models according to their integration of praxis. But it might also be possible to stress the basic agreement of these two sets of models regarding the problematic of contemporary fundamental theology. The five models of Lamb fall into the three categories of assimiation, isolation, or dialogue.[43] Dialogue is the most fruitful relationship.

Assimilation	Isolation	Dialogue
orthodox	neo-orthodox	revisionist
paleomorphic	fideomorphic	criticomorphic
		politicomorphic
liberal		
radical		
neomorphic		

A confrontational theology demands an isolation which, as we have seen, is dangerous to both religion and its cultural partner. Assimilation is the identification of faith and culture in which one partner of the mediation translates and reformulates the other into its terms. It is an attempt to mediate both sides of the dialectic in terms proper to one side. Dialogue is here used in a special sense to indicate a true mediation in which each listens in openness to the other and respects its integrity. Neither side has an automatic advantage. In various ways models of isolation and assimilation finally offer only a monologue. Both Lamb and Tracy find this inadequate. There is no doubt that whatever else contemporary theology must be or avoid, it must be a theology of genuine dialogue and avoid falling into isolation or assimilation.

This concern over the proper model for fundamental theology indicates another view common in contemporary theology, viz., that fundamental theology is theology grown self-reflective. In any discipline there is a presupposed framework which determines not only what shall constitute a problem but also what shall constitute a solution.[44] The current interest in foundations is a result of a serious uncertainty about the paradigm for theology. Indeed, many feel that the question of an adequate paradigm for theology is the most important question facing contemporary theology. What is at stake is the very character of the discipline: what is theology, what modes of argument are appropriate to it, what methods are productive, what warrants convincing. Today it is common to look at the foundations of a theology before laboring over its content and conclusions. A logically and aesthetically impressive edifice may often prove to be an ill-grounded and hazardous shelter. Contemporary theology insists on the articulation of the explicit or implicit criteria operative in any particular theological approach.

A discussion of the foundations of theology will be a discussion of the method of inquiry proper to theology. Furthermore, it will be a discussion which presumes that these methods must be explicit and defensible. For a variety of reasons--including the present secularity, an infatuation with science, and a dazzling pluralism--the procedures and assumptions which allow and structure the theological enterprise must be publicly available and accountable. Facilitating a public conversation about our understanding of faith is the task of fundamental theology.

> For that reason, methodological reflection--or, as I prefer to call it, fundamental theological reflection--is not an academic pastime. Rather, it is pure necessity for adjudicating the warring claims of the theologies fighting for one's attention. Anyone who presents a "theology" presumably asks the rest of us to register our agreement. And yet, many present "theologies of . . . " seem to operate on the basis of "love me or leave me." Some of us would appreciate another option. The emancipatory and public character of critical reason promises to provide just that: public discourse, genuine communication; authentic conversion. The fundamental theologian's principal responsibility is to try to articulate the norms and procedures, the methods and the rules of evidence which would allow for that conversation.[45]

The paradigms for modern theology often conflict and diverge. The substantive conclusions of a theology depend greatly upon its method of inquiry. Awareness of the paradigm governing one's work is essential to a self-conscious and credible theology. At any rate, for what ever reasons, it seems that most contemporary fundamental theology is an attempt to work out "the basic criteria and methods for theological argument."[46]

The point of this chapter has been to provide a useful, though not strictly definitional, sense of what we are talking about when we claim to be doing fundamental or foundational theology. We have indicated some of the threads connecting foundational theology with the ongoing development of theology and culture. Some of the needs and contingencies which influence its present shape have been noted. An impression of the various modern responses which constitute it has been given. Tracking back and forth over the territory has provided a feel for the concerns of foundational theologians. For those who like a neater package, one might pull these threads together by recalling their general direction. Foundational theology focuses on method. More specifically, foundational theology is concerned with formulating a mediation of religion and culture which is dialogical. This is to be accomplished by the articulation and defense of the public criteria for any theological discourse. The entire project, as a working out of the method of inquiry proper to theology, is basically methodological. Of course the determination of the nature of this method remains a point of debate. It seems clear that theology should be revisionist in its attitude toward its sources and in its drive for credibility. It must be faithful both to the intellectual life and to the religious life. It also seems worthwhile to ask whether the foundations of theology can be purely theoretical. Such a synoptic glimpse of the forms and concerns of fundamental theology hardly provides a precise and universal definition of the discipline. Nevertheless, this imprecise descriptive approach will serve. It does provide a sense of direction.

What has Ludwig Wittgenstein to do with all this? This is the general theological context for the appropriation of his thought. Here is our point of contact. He offers us a philosophical perspective compatible with the present needs of philosophical theology. For Wittgenstein, doing philosophy is public and radically non-theoretical. His work is concerned with foundations, it is methodological, and it is praxis oriented. Attention to the thought of Ludwig Wittgenstein, then, may have significant implications for fundamental theology.

Yet many misread his work and misconstrue his usefulness. In fact, his approach is a rejection of "foundations" as usually understood in the history of philosophy. We offer here a close attention to the proper reading of Wittgenstein and a concrete example of how he can benefit fundamental theology. The procedure will not be to begin <u>ab novo</u> but to refine a sample of the best contemporary theology we can find. Specifically, we propose to study the revisionist foundations of David Tracy with a Wittgenstein eye. This will display the resources offered by the thought of the later Wittgenstein. The first move will be to understand Tracy's position and to surface the criteria operative in his theology. The second move will be to offer a Wittgensteinian critique. From Tracy's point of view, this is a revision of his revisionism. While the following pages are offered as a piece of foundational theology, they also constitute a criticism of the search for foundations.

There is a great advantage in doing a close study of one example. Whether Wittgenstein's linguistic method works or not can be seen at close range in a controlled conversation with a particular theology. If it is successful, the reader will himself confess this to be so and note the light it sheds on many other theologies. This is the Wittgensteinian approach. By taking a single example and examining it thoroughly, we hope to display a new pattern for theological method and a new perspective on the theological search for foundations.

Notes

1. Bernard J. F. Lonergan, Method in Theology (New York: Herder and Herder, 1972), p. xi. Although I do not slavishly adhere to Lonergan's perspective, I am inspired by him in what follows. His functional specialties (pp. 125-45) provide a convenient way to organize and locate foundations in respect to the other branches of theology. This general view is not limited to the Catholic discussion. There is a similar location of foundational or philosophical theology, for example, in Schubert Ogden, "What is Theology?" Journal of Religion 52 (January 1972):22-40.

2. For the historical development consult Avery Dulles, A History of Apologetics (New York: Corpus Books, 1971; Adolf Kolping, Fundamental-theologie, 2 vols. (Munster: Regensbery, 1968), 1:35-70; Yves Congar, A History of Theology (New York: Doubleday, 1968); Heinrich Stirnimann, "Erwägungen zur Fundamentaltheologie: Problematik, Grundfragen, Konzept," Freiburger Zeitschrift für Philosophie und Theologie 24 (1977):291-317. The best treatment of the rise of fundamental theology and its transformation into contemporary foundational theology is Francis Schüssler Fiorenza, Foundational Theology: Jesus and the Church (New York: Crossroad, 1984), pp. 249-284. A helpful review of the direction of fundamental theology, especially as it makes the contemporary turn in which human experience is a more important source for theology, is presented in Claude Geffré, A New Age in Theology, trans. Robert Shillenn with Francis McDonagh and Theodore L. Westow (New York: Paulist Press, 1974). For an example of this movement and the concomitant shift from apologetics to foundations in the Catholic context see the seminal work of Karl Rahner. An illuminating article on Rahner's contribution is Gerald McCool, "Karl Rahner and the Christian Philosophy of St. Thomas Aquinas," in Theology and Discovery: Essays in Honor of Karl Rahner, S.J., ed. William J. Kelly (Milwaukee: Marquette University Press, 1980) pp. 63-93. Note as well Langdon Gilkey, "Trends in Protestant Apologetics," in The Development of Fundamental Theology, ed. Johannes B. Metz, Concilium, vol. 46 (New York: Paulist Press, 1969), pp. 127-57. Other informative overviews include Henri Bouillard, "Human Experience as the Starting Point of Fundamental Theology," trans. Eileen O'Gorman, in The Church and the World, ed. Johannes B. Metz, Concilium, vol. 6 (New York: Paulist Press, 1965), pp. 79-91; Heinrich Fries, "From Apologetics to Fundamental Theology," trans. John Drury, in The Development of Fundamental Theology, ed. J.B. Metz, pp. 57-68; Heinrich Fries, "Fundamental Theology," Sacramentum Mundi, pp. 66-70.

3. Avery Dulles, "How Can Christian Faith be Justified?" Communio 2 (Winter 1975):343-56. For attention to the historical evidence see his History of Apologetics. The same insistence on the "apologetic imperative" is argued from a different perspective in Patrick J. Burns, "An Apologetic of Liberation and Fulfillment," Communio 2

(Winter 1975):323-42.

4. The faith of an attentive modern person is constantly challenged by our pluralist and secularized milieu and so an account of one's faith becomes a condition for the possibility of believing at all. "The theological answer must be determined by the permanent menace which is indissolubly linked to the faith itself. It must be guided by the conviction that the question of unbelief is first and foremost a question put by the believer himself" (Metz, "Apologetics," p. 69). For expansion of this theme of the believer as always simul fidelis et infidelis see Metz, "Unbelief as a Theological Problem," trans. Tarcisius Rattler, in Metz, Church, pp. 59-77. There is a related debate over whether apologetics is part of theology proper. By and large the issue is the role of faith in the development of theological warrants and grounds. For a treatment of the issues see Thomas B. Ommen, "The Preunderstanding of the Theologian," in Kelly, Theology and Discovery, pp. 231-61. One manifestation of this problem is the current discussion as to whether or not religious studies differs in method and concerns from theology. In actual practice I find this supposed distinction vacuous. Cf. Schubert M. Ogden, "Theology and Religious Studies: Their Difference and the Difference it Makes," Journal of the American Academy of Religion 46 (March 1978):3-17; Charles Davis, "The Reconvergence of Theology and Religious Studies," Studies in Religion 4 (1974-75):205-21.

5. For a treatment of the ongoing development of mind and its impact see Lonergan, Method, pp. 90-99 and Lonergan, "Theology in its New Context," in A Second Collection, ed. William Ryan and Bernard J. Tyrrell (Philadelphia: Westminster Press, 1974), pp. 55-67.

6. Lonergan, "Aquinas Today: Tradition and Innovation," Journal of Religion 55 (April 1975):169-72. See also Lonergan, "Dimensions of Meaning," in Collection, ed. F. E. Crowe (New York: Herder and Herder, 1967), pp. 252-67. Cf. David Tracy, The Achievement of Bernard Lonergan (New York: Herder and Herder, 1970), pp. 84-91. Lonergan relies on Herbert Butterfield, The Origins of Modern Science: 1300-1800 (rev. ed. New York: Free Press, 1965). A clear discussion of modern physics which supports this view is Gary Zukav, The Dancing Wu Li Masters: An Overview of the New Physics (New York: William Morrow and Company, 1979).

7. This discussion is admittedly general. Nevertheless, the term "classicist" and "empiricist" are handy tags for highlighting a real change in tenor and content. There is a conflict in paradigms and it generates conflicting theologies. The world cannot be metaphysical, static, and a-historical as well as empirical, dynamic, and historical. For further elaboration of these two cultures see Lonergan, "Belief: Today's Issue," in A Second Collection, pp. 87-99.

8. A crisis in the meaning and certainty of doctrine is a major effect of cultural shift. Cf. Lonergan, "Philosophy and Theology," in The

Impact of Belief, ed. George F. McLean (Lancaster, Penn.: Concorde Publishing Company, 1974), pp. 36-43, and Lonergan, Doctrinal Pluralism (Milwaukee: Marquette University Press, 1971). For a helpful perspective on the problem of dogma in light of this challenge see Thomas B. Ommen, The Hermeneutic of Dogma, American Academy of Religion Dissertation Series, no. 11 (Misoula, Montana: Scholars Press, 1975).

9. Theologians quarrel over which label best suggests the direction of their work. In our discussion these three terms are used interchangeably.

10. The warning of theologian Walter Kasper is typical: "We can no longer avoid discussing the principles and basic criteria of theological argumentation. Methodological examination of the foundations of theology is a most urgent task for post-conciliar Theology" (The Methods of Dogmatic Theology, trans. J. Drury (New York: Paulist Press, 1969), p. 4). For now, "method" indicates a cluster of issues revolving around the presentation of criteria for carrying on. A second important question is prescinded from: Given the validity of the general problem of method, does a theoretical version of method provide a sufficient solution?

11. One gets a further sense of the variety simply by working through, for example, Metz, Development. A useful and recent collection of articles is René Latourelle and Gerald O'Collins, eds., Problems and Perspectives of Fundamental Theology, trans. Mathew J. O'Connell (New York: Paulist Press, 1982). In addition note the positions of G. Sohngen, "Fundamentaltheologie," in Lexikon für Theologie und Kirche, 4th ed., cols. 452-59 and Henri Bouillard, The Logic of Faith, trans. M. H. Gill & Son (New York: Sheed and Ward, 1967), pp. 11-35. This diversity is increased by the whole group of theologians who have not even made the turn from the deductive objectivism of the old apologetics to an inductive, empirical, and anthropocentric foundations. A precise and universally acceptable definition for fundamental theology remains illusive. For a sense of this evolution and new directions see F. Fiorenza, Foundational Theology.

12. Van A. Harvey, The Historian and the Believer (New York: Macmillan Press, 1969), p. 127: " . . . the heart of the issue before us is the collision of two moralities of knowledge, the one characteristic of the scholarly world since the Enlightenment, the other characteristic of traditional Christian belief." This presentation of the contemporary apologetic task is the starting point for David Tracy's sketch of the theological landscape.

13. BRO, p. 23. The proximate inspiration for Tracy's notion of models is Bernard Lonergan. Taking Lonergan's notion of horizon analysis (cf. Tracy, Achievement, pp. 1-21), Tracy fuses it with Lonergan's view of models: "Models, then, stand to the human sciences, to philosophies, to theologies, much as mathematics stands to the natural sciences. For models purport to be, not descriptions of reality, not hypotheses about

reality, but simly interlocking sets of terms and relations." (Method, p. 284). Tracy is quite aware of the limits of any model, including his own disclosure models. "Such a distinction allows one to affirm that theological models do not purport to provide exact pictures of the realities they disclose (picture models). Rather, theological models serve to disclose or re-present the realities which they interpret. Theological disclosure models like the religious symbols upon which they reflect, in Reinhold Niebuhr's famous phrase, should be taken seriously but not literally. Theologies do not--or should not--claim to provide pictures of the realities they describe--God, humanity, and the world; they can be shown to disclose such realities with varying degrees of adequacy" (BRO, p. 22). For Tracy's sources in the literature on models see BRO, p. 34, n. 1.

14. BRO, p. 24. See also BRO, p. 35, n. 12: "The phrase 'inner-theological' suggests that all norms for theological statements are to be found in the 'authorities' affirmed by the particular church community, not by 'outside' communities of inquiry."

15. BRO, p. 24 provides a brief indication of this nuanced position. For a closer analysis which also attends to the historical impact and development see Gerald McCool, Catholic Theology in the Nineteenth Century: The Quest for a Unitary Method (New York: Seabury, 1977).

16. BRO, p. 26.

17. Tracy feels that Schleiermacher is the clearest example. Friedrich Schleiermacher, The Christian Faith, ed. H. R. Mackintosh and J. S. Steward (Edinburgh: T & T Clark, 1928); Schleiermacher, Brief Outline of the Study of Theology trans. Terrence N. Tice (Richmond: John Knox Press, 1966).

18. Typical works include Karl Barth, The Epistle to the Romans, trans. E. C. Hoskyns (London: Oxford University Press, 1960); Rudolf Bultmann, New Testament and Mythology and Other Basic Writings, selected, edited, and translated by Schubert M. Ogden (Philadelphia: Fortress Press, 1984); Paul Tillich, Systematic Theology, 3 vols. (Chicago: University of Chicago Press, 1951-1953); Reinhold Niebuhr, The Nature and Destiny of Man, 2 vols. (New York: Scribner, 1949).

19. BRO, p. 28.

20. BRO, p. 31. Thomas Altizer and William Hamilton, Radical Theology and the Death of God (Indianapolis: Bobbs-Merrill, 1966); Thomas J. Altizer, The Gospel of Christian Atheism (Philadelphia: Westminster, 1966); Paul van Buren, The Secular Meaning of the Gospel (New York: Macmillan, 1963).

21. BRO, pp. 32-33. Besides Tracy himself, examples of a revisionist approach would also include Gregory Baum, Man Becoming:

God in Secular Experience (New York: Herder and Herder, 1970); Michael Novak, Ascent of the Mountain, Flight of the Dove: An Invitation to Religious Studies (New York: Harper & Row, 1971); Langdon Gilkey, Naming the Whirlwind: The Renewal of God-Language (Indianapolis: Bobbs-Merrill, 1969); Gordon D. Kaufman, God the Problem (Cambridge, Massachusetts: Harvard University Press, 1972); Kaufman, An Essay on Theological Method (Missoula, Montana: Scholars Press, 1975); Schubert M. Ogden, The Reality of God (New York: Harper & Row, 1969).

22. This delicate balance of reciprocal criticism is seen in revisionism's characteristic insistence on the distinction between the secularity it champions and a deadly, myopic secularism. When he embraces secularity, the modern theologian is embracing that nexus of concepts and method which define true knowledge and which structure and drive the spirit of our age. But when these conceptions and this method become truncated and twisted by an interpretation which precludes transcendence, then this liberating secularity has become a constraining secularism. While secularity may be an aid to mediation, secularism by definition rules out any real theological mediation. For an excellent elaboration of this secular spirit and an attack on any secularistic interpretation of secularity see Gilkey, Whirlwind, especially pp. 31-71 and 305-413.

23. Matthew L. Lamb, History, Method and Theology: A Dialectical Comparision of Wilhelm Dilthey's Critique of Historical Reason and Bernard Lonergan's Meta-Methodology, with a forward by Bernard Lonergan, American Academy of Religion Dissertation Series, no. 25 (Missoula, Montana: Scholars Press, 1978), pp. 2-54. The models are refined with even more stress to praxis in Lamb, "The Theory-Praxis Relationship in Contemporary Christian Theologies," Catholic Theological Society of American Proceedings 31 (June 1976):149-78; Lamb, Solidarity with Victims: Toward a Theology of Social Transformation (New York: Crossroad Publishing Co., 1982) pp. 61-99.

24. Lamb, "Theory-Praxis," p. 157. For a fuller characterization of paleomorphic culture see Lamb, History, Method and Theology, pp. 10-16.

25. For a careful study of the origins and influences of this theology of the magisterium, a theology which has shaped many American bishops and generated a good bit of post-conciliar conflict, see T. Howland Sanks, Authority in the Church: A Study in Changing Paradigms (Missoula, Montana: Scholars Press, 1974). A brief presentation can be found in Sanks, "Co-operation, Co-option, Condemnation: Theologians and the Magisterium 1870-1978," Chicago Studies 17 (Summer 1978):242-263.

26. Lamb, "Theory-Praxis," p. 164.

27. Lamb, History, Method and Theology, p. 22. Catholics tend to

stress the former, Protestants the latter. Charismatics of any stripe are another example of those who find fideomorphism an acceptable refuge from relativism.

28. Barth, Epistle; Hans Urs von Balthasar, Love Alone trans. and ed. Alexander Dru (New York: Herder and Herder, 1969); von Balthasar, Word and Redemption, trans. A. V. Littledale with Alexander Dru (New York: Herder and Herder, 1965); Peter Berger and Richard Neuhaus, eds., Against the World for the World: The Hartford Appeal and the Future of American Religion (New York: Seabury, 1976). Note that while Tracy classes Bultmann with Barth, Lamb separates them. Lamb distinguishes Bultmann, Tillich and Rahner as non-fideomorphic because they accept the need to relate critical historical method and faith.

29. "Perhaps the most difficult task these theologians have engaged in is their effort at articulating the critical normative unity of identity and non-identity. They do not find that normative unity of critique in classical culture, as does the paleomorphic, nor in the 'progressive' elements of contemporary culture as do the neomorphic, nor in an exclusive reliance upon the word of God, as do the fideomorphic. They seek rather to find that normative unity in the interaction between faith and reason, between theology and culture, that will be consonant with both the demands of faith and the aspirations of contemporary mankind" (Lamb, History, Method and Theology) p. 23.

30. Lamb, "Theory-Praxis," p. 166.

31. These mediational theologians set up a correlation between Historie and Geschichte, the categorical and the transcendent, the ontological and the ontic. Cf. Lamb, "Theory-Praxis," pp.166-68. For a full development see Lamb, History, Method and Theology, pp. 22-30.

32. Lamb, "Theory-Praxis," p. 171.

33. Lamb, History, Method and Theology, pp. 31 and 41-53.

34. For an indication of the value of critical theory see Matthew L. Lamb, Solidarity, pp. 28-60. A brief introduction to critical theory is Tom Bottomore, The Frankfort School (New York: Tavistock Publications, 1984). For a more substantial discussion consult David Held, Introduction to Critical Theory: Horkheimer to Habermas (Berkley: University of California Press, 1980). Metz gives some indication of the impact of this school upon his theology in "Political Theology," Sacramentum Mundi, pp. 34-38. The fullest treatment of political theology as fundamental theology is Metz, Faith in History and Society: Toward a Practical Fundamental Theology, trans. David Smith (New York: Seabury Press, 1980). Cf. Lamb, History, Method and Theology, pp. 30-53.

35. Lamb, "Theory-Praxis," p. 171. "Only a critical theory, that is a theorizing which is attentive to its own operations as praxis and open

to correction in the light of that praxis, can free methodology, philosophy, the sciences, and technology from present dehumanizations in society and ecology" (Lamb, Solidarity, p. 41).

36. For the background to the issue of praxis refer to Richard J. Bernstein, Praxis and Action: Contemporary Philosophies of Human Activity (Philadelphia: University of Pennsylvania Press, 1971); Nicholas Lobkowicz, Theory and Practice: History of a Concept from Aristotle to Marx (Notre Dame: University of Notre Dame Press, 1967); Jurgen Habermas, Theory and Practice (Boston: Beacon Press, 1973); W. Post, "Theory and Practice," in Sacramentum Mundi, pp. 246-49. "Theory is the consciouness of praxis; praxis is action infused with and made conscious by theory. Marx rejected the notion of theory independent of praxis, theory as presuppositionless, contemplative recognition of a stable object. Indeed, any theory claiming such independence was ideology, all the more mystifying reflection of existing society, the more it claimed an illusory independence. . . . Further, while critical theory infused revolutionary praxis and made it conscious, the transformation effected by praxis in turn changed theory by altering its basis. Theory and praxis march in step" Charles Davis, "Theology and Praxis," Cross Currents 23 (Summer 1973):159-60.

37. Lamb, "Theory-Praxis," p. 173. Cf. William Shea, "Matthew Lamb's Five Models of Theory-Praxis and the Interpretation of John Dewey's Pragmatism," Catholic Theological Society of America Proceedings 32 (June 1977):134-35.

38. Lamb, History, Method and Theology, p. 45; Lamb, Solidarity, pp. 39-41.

39. For Lamb, this method is the cognitional theory-praxis of self-appropriation discovered by B. Lonergan: "Since authentic praxis can never be taken for granted, and since the critical problem can never be solved by theories qua theories, Lonergan has thematized a radical cognitive therapy aimed at a basic liberation of the human subject through a heightening of awareness which appropriates the structures of experiencing, understanding, judging, deciding." Lamb, "Theory-Praxis," p. 174. Cf. Lonergan, Insight: A study of Human Understanding, 3rd ed. (New York: Philosophical Library, 1970) pp. ix-316; Lonergan, "Cognitional Structure," in Collection, pp. 221-39.

40. Again, method here is not a theory of relationships or a step-by-step technique. Rather method indicates the action-oriented theory-praxis feedback character of praxis. For further treatment of political theology as basically this type of method as distinct from the more static historical-philosophical criticomorphic mediation, see Lamb, "Les implications méthodologiques de la théologie politique: Essai pour surmonter la crise de la théologie comme science," in Marcel Xhaufflaire, ed., La Pratique de la théologie politique (Tournai: Casterman, 1974) pp. 51-70.

41. Lamb, "Theory-Praxis," pp. 169-70.

42. BRO, p. 242. Tracy does not criticize Lamb's own theology. However, Lamb does criticize Tracy's attack on political theology in Lamb, "Theory-Praxis," p. 164, n. 55. For a more extensive indication of Lamb's reply to charges of neo-orthodoxy issued by Tracy, see Lamb, "Dogma, Experience and Political Theology," in Revelation and Experience, ed. Edward Schillebeeckx and Bas van Iersel, Concilium, vol. 113 (New York: Seabury, 1979), pp. 79-90. The position is refined in Solidarity. Lamb's suggestion that Tracy is naive in his understanding of political theology seems to have had an impact. Tracy mollifies his charge of neo-orthodoxy and takes extensive note of Lamb's views in his brief discussion of praxis and theology in David Tracy, The Analogical Imagination: Christian Theology and the Culture of Pluralism (New York: Crossroad Publishing Co., 1981), pp. 69-82, 390-98. However, it would not be correct to say that Tracy has now appropriated Lamb's critique. Tracy's solution remains fundamentally theoretical.

43. Although I have modified their names, the idea for these three categories is borrowed from Xhaufflaire, Feuerbach et la théologie de la sécularisation (Paris: Les Editions du Cerf, 1970), pp. 307-39. Lamb and Tracy might well charge that my modeling of their models is essentialist. It de-emphasize the differing axes proper to each set of models. However, with this caveat in mind, my models do effectively stress the agreement of Lamb and Tracy on a picture of theology as open, public and unrestricted inquiry. Furthermore, they do indicate why some of the models fail to provide an adequate mediation. There is a sense of direction in contemporary fundamental theology.

44. Cf. Thomas S. Kuhn, The Structure of Scientific Revolutions, 2nd ed. (Chicago: University of Chicago Press, 1970).

45. Tracy, "Theology as Public Discourse," Christian Century March 1975, p. 281.

46. BRO, p. 15.

CHAPTER TWO
A REVISIONIST FOUNDATION:
THE THEOLOGY OF DAVID TRACY

The Project: Meaningfulness, Truth, and Correlation

In our age of secularity and pluralism, fundamental theology becomes a quest for some sort of critical control in a sea of complex and conflicting claims. Such control cannot be found in an appeal to some standard outside or above the present cacophony. Rather we must look inside to the heart of the various positions and counter-positions which vie for affirmation; we must look to foundations. For David Tracy, fundamental theology is a search for the foundational criteria of theological argument. What criteria, what standards, do we appropriately invoke in theological discourse? Such a question may come to rest on several levels. Tracy moves his investigation to the level of the most essential and fundamental criteria in any discourse: those of meaning and truth. What is it for a statement to have meaning in theology? What is it for a statement to be true in theology? These questions determine what counts as part of an argument and what does not; they reveal the bedrock of any theological enterprise. Tracy discusses these questions as a foundation for theology in his brilliant Blessed Rage for Order[1].

Thus theology is shaped by the present context of theological inquiry. As Tracy sees it, the contemporary challenge to theology has taken the form of an attack upon both the existential and the cognitive claims of the Christian tradition. The modern problem is largely an Enlightenment inheritance: an unbounded faith in the power of autonomous reason to liberate us for full humanity has issued in an uncritical prescinding from the riches of the religious perspective. As this new reason developed new sciences, these sciences in turn developed a textual, historical, psychological, scientific and philosophical critique of religion. This demystification, as we have seen, was necessary and inevitable. But will it finally forge a refined Christian view of God and man, or will it find the Christian fact to be existentially and intellectually vacuous? Can the modern person really experience the Christian world-view as meaningful? Do Christian symbols survive a critical intellectual analysis of their reality? In the face of this existential and cognitive challenge of modernity, the Christian theologian discovers a concomitant professional and ethical duty to assess the tradition in terms of its claims to existential meaningfulness and cognitive truth.[2] The contemporary theologian must "provide evidence to fair-minded critics inside and outside Christianity for the meaning and truth of the central Christian symbols."[3]

This conception of the fundamental theologian's task in the modern world generates the revisionist's conception of fundamental theology as a philosophical analysis focused on meaning. Philosophy has long had a privileged and integral place in theologizing, and it has developed some useful tools for the analysis of meaning. Although Tracy will appeal to other relevant disciplines such as literary criticism and critical history, the thrust of his quest for criteria of meaning and truth falls within the traditional scope of philosophy. As a theological enterprise, such a philosophical examination will have to look not only to our strictly secular experience of being human, but also to the record of explicitly religious experience found in Christian scripture and tradition. The "meanings" contained therein, in both our common human experiences and our Christian sources, will be the precise target of this philosophical examination.

> In its briefest expression, the revisionist model holds that a contemporary fundamental Christian theology can best be described as philosophical reflection upon the meanings present in common human experience and language, and upon the meanings present in thee Christian fact.[4]

Foundational theology, then, is an analysis of meaning utilizing the best philosophical tools available. For this reason the problem of how to locate these "meanings" and whether they are true occupies the major portion of <u>Blessed Rage for Order</u>.

Revisionist fundamental theology is primarily concerned with the criteria for meaning and truth in theological discourse. These criteria are the foundation for theology. Before taking up the specifics of Tracy's view of meaning, truth, and foundations, it would be well to review the broad outline of his version of revisionism.

Tracy sets the context of a contemporary theology as one of pluralism and secularity. He affirms that in such a setting theology needs to meet the same intellectual ethic as the other scholarly disciplines, and yet must do so in such a way that it preserves its characteristic insistence on the human person as <u>homo religious</u>. The proper unification of these two concerns is the task of a critical Christian fundamental theology. For Tracy the key to this unification is the conviction that the secular faith we all share and Christian faith can be seen as different articulations of what he and Schubert Ogden call our "basic faith." Hence on the one hand religion has nothing to fear from the best secular methods of inquiry, for these tools merely help us to find this same basic faith beneath their own special areas. On the other hand, our secular faith is not negated by religious faith, but rather is well expressed by it. The thesis that there is one basic faith sustaining the various particular (religious or secular) instances of that faith locates a unity within our pluralism and allows a fruitful interplay between religious consciousness and the scientific community of scholars. Secular criteria and pluralism can be embraced by theology. Theological integrity does not require special pleading. Theology can become a public discourse.

Tracy must next specify his own brand of revisionism. He draws the lineaments of his particular model by proposing five theses. For purposes of our exposition, his theses can be grouped into the three distinct but related operations of investigation, correlation and validation.

Correlation is the focus of Tracy's first two theses. These theses set the premise that theology is the correlation of Christian texts with common human experience.

> First Thesis: The Two Principle Sources for Theology are Christian Texts and Common Human Experience and Language.[5]

> Second Thesis: The Theological Task Will Involve a Critical Correlation of the Results of the Investigation of the Two Sources of Theology.[6]

In this correlation, each pole must be measured by the other and the theologian must be faithful to both. In other words, there are two preliminary criteria for theological statements: appropriateness and adequacy. One's theological categories must be appropriate (i.e., must allow clear access) to the meanings of the Christian tradition (the Christian fact). There would, after all, be no point in a Christian theology which negated the major motifs of Christianity. But one's theology must also provide an adequate interpretation of common human experience, for Christianity claims to be the authentic understanding of all human experience.[7] This claim implies the necessity of correlating two factors and presupposes a refined notion of each. One must understand human experience and then show the relation between it and Christian tradition.

This insistence that the terms for theologizing be adequate to our common human experience and appropriate to the Christian fact is a prerequisite for Tracy's demand that the relation of these terms be a truly critical correlation. The adequacy of the Christian tradition to common experience is not to be shown by the half-hearted (though not uncommon) sort of correlation which matches the question of secular experience with the answers of religious experience.[8] Rather, both the questions and the answers of common human experience are to be taken seriously. A true correlation must place the questions and answers found in the Christian tradition in dialogue with the questions and the answers suggested by our common secular experience. The idea of an honest correlation contains the whole revisionist project, for it demands theological criteria and methods which are both appropriate to the Christian texts and adequate to our common human experience. It respects the integrity and wholeness of each source and yet demands the correlation of its peculiar meaning. But, while this framework of correlation is, in a sense, logically prior, its operation is empirically second. Before the actual correlation can take place, one must surface the meanings present in each of these sources. This largely phenomenological task constitutes the next grouping of revisionist operations as investigative.

Theses three and four ask what method will be most suitable for the accurate description of the "meanings" discovered within each of our theological resources. What procedure can be adequate and appropriate? It is concluded that, at present, phenomenology provides the best tool for the liberation of meaning.

> Third Thesis: The Principle Method of Investigation of the Source "Common Human Experience and Language" Can Be Described as a Phenomenology of the "Religious Dimension" Present in Everyday and Scientific Experience and Language.[9]

> Fourth Thesis: The Principle Method of Investigation of the Source "The Christian Tradition" Can Be Described as an Historical and Hermeneutical Investigation of Classical Christian Texts.[10]

Tracy will specify the particular sort of phenomenology to be used later. For now, he simply uses the word generically to argue that the theologian must analyze and explicate the phenomena (i.e., the data which appear immediately to consciousness) which compose our two sources. He is confident that such an investigation can discover the self-understanding or horizon which generates and is thematized in our common human experience and the Christian tradition. He calls for a mode of philosophical reflection that can display the preconceptual, pre-thematic dimension not only of our shared experience and language, but also of the New Testament witness. Of course, given the historical complexity and distance of the New Testament evidence, Tracy advocates that a critical historical study of these texts precede his hermeneutic phenomenology of this pole. Only after the general sense of the text is reconstructed can the theologian disclose the referents implicit in its horizon.[11] Common human experience and Christian symbols, then, are both subject to some sort of phenomenological x-ray. The purpose of such an examination is to disclose the experience which provides the meaning of each theological source. Note that the entree to each pole is its linguistic expression: the meaning to be found at the pre-thematic, pre-linguistic level is liberated by the phenomenological examination of language. Tracy's search for meaning has become a linguistic phenomenology of our human and religious experience.

This investigation of the two sources for theology surfaces a special dimension (named the religious) present in both common human experience and scripture. When this disclosure of the referent of the Christian text and of our common human experience is complete, there remain the final movements of Tracy's fundamental theological procedure: the actual correlation of these meanings and the matter of their truth.

While the investigative moment is phenomenological, the final correlation—the comparision and subsequent validation—of meaning is metaphysical or transcendental. Phenomenological philosophical reflection produces an understanding of theology's two sources by piercing through the superficial and disclosing the underlying meaning. Comparision of this phenomenological description of each pole reveals an identical basic faith experience grounding both. This shared basic faith is found to provide the "ultimate or grounding dimension or horizon to all meaningful human activities."[12] Further, such an ultimate grounding horizon is exactly the sort of experience which Tracy wishes to designate as "religious." Common human experience and the Christian tradition are rooted in an identical, basically religious, faith horizon and hence both can be said to present (in their own ways, of course) religious meaning. But correlation must move beyond comparison to validation: Tracy also wants to know whether these meanings are true. Is the experience of the religious/basic faith dimension related to any object or referent? Is that referent real? Do the meanings present in the two sources of theology imply the same referent? The question <u>quid sit</u> (what is it) naturally propels him to the question <u>an sit</u> (whether it is).

> Fifth Thesis: To Determine the Truth-Status of the Results of One's Investigation into the Meaning of Both Common Human Experience and Christian Texts, The Theologian Should Employ Explicitly Transcendental or Metaphysical Modes of Reflection.[13]

A phenomenological mode of reflection reveals the same religious horizon beneath common human experience and The Christian fact, but a metaphysical mode of reflection is required to affirm the necessary referent of that basic faith, and to show that this referent is properly called theistic.

Metaphysics, for Tracy, is a Kantian sort of transcendental occupation, a search for "the ground, the basis, the fundament of every phenomenon which appears to human consciousness."[14] It is a concern with ultimate presupposition, with the conditions for the possibility of the phenomenon under consideration. Now the religious horizon, for Tracy, is defined as the most basic and universal condition of all human knowing and experience. Because the religious (by definition) claims to be ultimate ground of all meaningful human activity, it must account not just for some particular experience, but for the roots of all experience. The discipline needed to verify its cognitive claims must be one of transcendental reflection, one concerned with the "basic presuppositions (or 'beliefs') that are the condition of the possibility of our existing or understanding at all."[15] The nature of religion as ultimacy requires a validating mode of reflection geared to the discovery of ultimate presuppositions. Metaphysics is such a discipline.[16] Phenomenology can disclose and articulate our experience; metaphysics can disclose and articulate the origins of that experience. The ultimate grounding horizon of all meaningful human action was found to be a religious dimension, and now the reality of this dimension is found to be validated by the necessity of its referent. This referent may be named "God." The final moment of revisionism insists that one is compelled to see "the concepts 'religion' and 'God' as necessarily affirmed or necessarily denied by all our basic beliefs and understanding."[17]

This insistence on the need for a metaphysics is, at this point, not so much an appeal to a particular metaphysical view as a realization that meaningfulness and truth are separate conditions requiring differing criteria. In general, a phenomenology reveals to us a certain self-understanding within our experience, while a metaphysics discloses the conditions for the possibility of that experienced self-understanding.[18] The method suitable for the liberation of meaning is not that useful for the intellectual validation of that meaning's truth. A fundamental theology which is centered on a quest for meaning and truth must include, in some sense of the terms, a phenomenology and a metaphysic.

In the exposition of these five theses, Tracy outlines revisionism as philosophical reflection on the meanings present in common human experience and the Christian fact. He explains his notion of philosophical reflection by reviewing the methods he would use for the investigation of meanings and for their correlation and validation. The following emerge as hallmarks of Tracy's project: (1) The criteria and methodology employed in doing theology must be public and must meet the standards which ordinarily govern the community of scholars. (2) Revisionism is a critical communion of two sources, one explicitly religious and the other not explicitly religious. This communion is such that eventually the secular is seen to be religious and the religious to be secular and hence their terminological distinction is seen to be less accurate and less fundamental than is often supposed. (3) The "meanings" with which Tracy is concerned turn out to be the horizon of self-understanding which provides (though not prima facie) the determinative structure for the phenomena of both poles. Tracy's use of the term "philosophical reflection" is limited to what can broadly be called a phenomenological-transcendental mode of reflection. This is the way--a phenomenological investigation and a metaphysical validation--in which Tracy will approach the crucial revisionist issues of meaning and truth. Meaning is found when the immediacy of that basic faith which grounds and is mediated by symbolic and conceptual phenomena (among other manifestations) is liberated to consciousness by the study of those phenomenal carriers.[19] The truth of this perceived meaning (or phenomenally mediated immediacy) is discovered by asking what must be the case for such a horizon to be experienced.

By now one has a fairly good idea of Tracy's method, i.e., what sort of philosophical reflection will be applied to what sort of meanings as found in which sources. The task of investigation is to liberate the pre-linguistic experience grounding each pole by piercing through the expression of that experience. Tracy will adopt a phenomenology of our common human experience and language patterned on the work of Langdon Gilkey and a hermeneutic phenomenology of the New Testament derived from the thought of Paul Ricoeur. The correlation of the results of this phenomenology begins when the criteria which are adequate for one pole and those appropriate to the other are applied to their opposite pole. It is found that the language which mediates the immediacy of their common religious dimension can be characterized as limit language. The task of this limit language is to hematize its originating horizon. Conceptual and symbolic statements are working properly and are to be judged meaningful inasmuch as they mediate this basic faith dimension to consciousness. Finally, the study of meaningfulness leads one to raise the question of the metaphysical character of its referent. Tracy finds that "theistic" is a good way to describe a necessary referent of this sort.

Religious claims that are related well to experience may be properly called meaningful for Tracy. If they are also logically coherent they have what Tracy distinguishes as meaning. In order to be true they must be seen as fundamental to all experience. Phenomenology demonstrates that the meanings of both poles can be named "religious" and metaphysics shows that the title "theistic" best describes their necessary and originating referent. Revisionism can be seen as the development of standards to govern the theological application of the terms meaning, meaningful and true. Furthermore, both of these methods are an appeal to experiential criteria: in the end theological sources must submit to the critically mediated experience of the self. Thus the revisionist method is linguistic and empirical; it shows the proper use of terms by highlighting our experience.[20] Revisionism wishes to demonstrate that there are experiential grounds for affirming the meaning, meaningfulness, and truth of the "religious" and "theistic" interpretation of our most fundamental human experience.[21] All of this is aimed at developing a public theology. The first part of Blessed Rage for Order thus provides us with a prescription for the revisionist project in general and for Tracy's version of it in particular.

The substantive conclusions of these methods of investigation and validation are elaborated in the remaining chapters of the book. There one finds two chapters on the actual meanings present in common human experience and Christian texts, two chapters on their truth, and two chapters on the relation of these criteria for meaning and truth to other branches of theology. It is an ever widening circle of interpretation moving from the basic experience of a religious dimension discovered in both common human experience and religious experience (chapters five and six respectively), to the metaphysical-theistic verification and interpretation of this dimension (chapters seven and eight), and its thematization in systematic theology (chapter nine's example of Christology) and in practical theology (chapter ten's notes on a social ethic). Of the six chapters which comprise the second part of <u>Blessed Rage for Order</u>, four pay special attention to the fundamental theologian's search for meaning and truth.

The point of this review has been to show that Tracy's revisionist fundamental theology is characterized by its concern with meaning and truth as the foundational criteria of theology. <u>Blessed Rage for Order</u> began with a definition of revisionism as philosophical reflection on the meanings present in theology's two sources. This concern with meaning and truth continues to permeate the organization of the whole book and to influence each chapter. The five theses of revisionism pull this concern into a theological project which can be expressed as investigation of meaning, correlation of meaning, and validation of meaning. In each moment the concern with meaning remains while the emphasis shifts from locating the meanings, to the proper methods for revealing meaning, to establishing the sameness of these meanings and verifying their truth. These three moments take the specific form of a phenomenological getting clear on our basic experience and a transcendental look at the very conditions for the possibility of that experience. Our point of entry is language and our final criterion is experience. These empirical and linguistic operations comprise the search for meaning and truth which is the driving force of David Tracy's revisionist theology.

If meaning and truth are the central concerns of fundamental theology, then the criteria for meaning and truth are the foundation of that theology. There is no doubt that these two foci are the key to Tracy's revisionism. Yet exactly what he means by meaning and truth is still somewhat ambiguous. What are the relevant criteria? How do they actually determine meaning and truth? What sort of foundation do we have? A portrait of Tracy's criteria for meaning will include the nature of our basic faith experience, the ways it can ground our phenomenology and metaphysic, and the precise type of language involved in its expression. In order to display his view of the foundations of theology fully, let us now expand our simple sketch of Tracy's concern with meaning and truth into a more detailed picture of the criteria operative within this concern.

The Root of David Tracy's Revisionism: Basic Faith

The possibility and nature of the entire revisionist project rests upon the conviction that the thinking and the symbolizing, the reflection and the imagination, the philosophy and the religion characteristic of being human are rooted in a spontaneous pre-reflective faith. A single shared primal faith gives rise to diverse expressions. This is the epistemology which sets the framework for revisionism. It allows Tracy to deal with the problems of cultural shift and cultural relativity. It allows him to construct a public theology. It provides for a guarantee of the meaningfulness of religious discourse. A particular understanding of basic faith and its operation structures his picture of foundational theology.

It is always one's faith stance which finally "determines one's cognitive beliefs and one's individual ethical actions."[22] Faith, for Tracy, is a basic attitude and orientation, a primal and often non-conceptual stance toward reality. A belief is the explication or thematization of this faith.[23] Faith is prior, primitive, unthematic, and therefore more universal; beliefs are derivative, conceptual, structured and particular to their historical setting. A single faith may yield many beliefs. On this pattern, both philosophy and theology are the extrapolations of the particular beliefs implicitly entailed in a more basic faith. It follows that a critique of our beliefs, whether of our secular or of our religious beliefs, will investigate and validate those beliefs by reference to their one originating faith. At bottom, our basic pre-reflective faith is the source as well as the measure of both reflective thought and religious symbol.

It is the insistence on the pre-reflective source of all thought, symbol and language which, when applied to theological concerns, allows the critical correlation and mutual criticism so characteristic of revisionism. The possibility of a correlation of secular language and experience and religious language and experience becomes fairly unproblematic if both are viewed as attempts to express a faith they hold in common. The two sources of theology are, if anchored in the same pre-thematic experience, already correlated or identified at the deepest level. It is not a problem of whether there can be any correlation, for a theology which presumes the ultimate identity of its sources does not demonstrate the possibility of correlation but derives from it.[24]

If all thought is anchored in the same basic faith, there can be no problem demanding that religious reflection submit to the same criteria as other modes of thought. It is hardly startling for Tracy to insist that in working out their correlation both secular reflective thought and critical theology must be subject to the same criteria. In his view, both are accountable to the same source and seek the faithful formulation of that source. Both therefore are judged by criteria developed to measure fidelity to their common faith. The program of revisionism can be seen as attention to and understanding of the basic faith beneath our lives.

The notion of basic faith directs and delimits Tracy's search for foundations as a search for criteria of fidelity and correlation. To measure that fidelity is the duty of revisionist investigation, correlation and validation. Finding that a thematization--secular or religious--of this ultimate faith dimension is experientially and reflectively sufficient (i.e., meaningful, coherent and true) requires the finding and operation of an accurate phenomenology and an adequate metaphysics.[25] Furthermore, since each pole of theology, if it is faithful to its shared source, will correlate with the other, the success of the correlation itself is an additional criterion for fidelity. There is a sort of collateral verification: if two expressions of the same faith can be correlated in certain intellectual terms, then this increases the probability that these expressions are accurate accounts of their one originating faith. Of course this whole procedure implicity assumes that the philosophical terms which mediate the correlation (for Tracy the terms of phenomenological-transcendental reflection) are appropriate, i.e., that they can liberate meaning and truth. There is also the supposition that language is merely the mediator for the experiential criteria. The implications of these suppositions for the nature and value of revisionism will be taken up later. For now we have simply noted the formal role played by primal faith in setting the scope and operation of revisonist theology: it is the criterion for meaning and truth.

What is this common faith, shared by secularist and Christian theologian alike, which sets our theological problematic? It is that "faith in secularity" by which all human beings live, a "fundamental attitude which affirms the ultimate significance and final worth of our lives, our thought, and actions, here and now in nature and history."[26] It is this unshakeable confidence in the goodness of life, implied by all our cognitive and practical affairs, which allows us to carry on. Our basic faith is a foundational trust in the value of our ordinary, secular lives, a "basic confidence or assurance simply as human beings that life is worth living."[27] This faith appears in the positive adjustment of the individual being to the given, larger world in which it finds itself.

From this point of view, even animals have a confidence that their environment is supportive of their drive to live and reproduce.[28] The human too is seen to be part of a larger and given world in which it must have confidence to live. But human acceptance and adjustment require the additional element of reflective understanding. The vitality of the human animal rises above instinct and consciousness to the level of self-consciousness: its adjustment and acceptance cannot be merely a matter of instinct but must be a free, responsible and reasonable activity. For mankind to exist by faith is to accept one's life and its setting and to adjust oneself to them in a self-conscious and reflective manner. But there is a level where reflective grounding ends. We must simply affirm and presume the unconditional validity and worth of life. We discover that our norms for living are rooted in a basic confidence in the worth of our ordinary lives; we discover our basic faith. Our characteristic human posture is receptive, listening and affirmative. This foundational and gracious experience of worth is what Tracy's theological investigations find in both religious texts and common human experience.

Tracy seeks to validate his claims by asking his readers to recall their own experience in the light of his conceptual and existential hints. The theology is empirical: any human being is in a position to verify its claims vis a vis his or her own experience of basic faith. It would be correct to label the appeal to such foundations as an appeal to experience. But one must be clear on just what Tracy means by experience. His appeal to experience is not another attempt to found knowing on some clear and distinct bit of data. On the contrary, he insists that we go deeper and look to the antecedent experience out of which such discrete data are differentiated. Basic faith is not one experience among others, but that which allows us to differentiate and distinguish any experience. The claims of such a basic dimension are not about the details of our experience but are concerned with its essential structure, with the wider experience of reality that makes any particular experience even possible. This means that sense perception and its consequent understanding are not the grounds but are themselves grounded in a more fundamental experience. The classical obsession with substance and qualities (or their equivalent) is misplaced. The usual doctrine of the primacy of sense perception is wrong-headed. To quote Whitehead: "Experience has been explained in a thoroughly topsy-turvy fashion, the wrong end first."[29]

> The whole notion of our massive experience conceived as a reaction to clearly envisaged details is fallacious. The relationship should never be inverted. The details are a reaction to the totality. They add definition. . . . They are interpretive and not originative. What is original is the vague totality.[30]

If this is Tracy's appeal to experience, it is not to the usual sort of experience. Since for him there is no value in seeking one's foundations in an appeal to sense experience or its clear and distinct understanding, Tracy's work is a radically different type of appeal to experience. He refers us to the non-sensuous experience of the self as a self and therein finds a grounding faith.

The basic confidence discovered at the root of human knowing and doing is not surfaced by attention to some world separate from our ego, to some isolated objective sphere encountered by an isolated subject. Rather, Tracy, like many others who are calling for a "turn to the subject," suspects the primacy and even the existence of a separable "already-out-there-now-real" and instead considers so-called objective reality to be a function of the subject.[31] An absolute partition between the subjective and the real is naive. Tracy accepts what Whitehead calls the "subjectivist principle," namely "that the whole universe consists of elements disclosed in the analysis of the experience of subjects."[32] This means that philosophy must focus on the experiencing self (the subject), not on the sense perception of objects: its task is the construction of a reflective <u>self</u>-understanding.

For Tracy, our experience of self is our most immediate

experience of the universe. Such an appeal to the self does not posit the experience of a subject over against that of an object or even over against itself as object. Neither sense data nor any internal psychological surrogate is sufficient. Tracy claims to appeal to a more basic mode of awareness than sensation. It is an appeal to the self as experiencing, i.e., to the kaleidoscopic overlapping of our non-objective experience of self. A sensationalist may refer us to the reports of our own five senses, but a non-sensationalist like Tracy refers us to an intuitive, non-sensuous experience of the self. Those who accept the sensationalist notion of experience verify their claims on the traditional pattern of scientific experiment which attempts to control and replicate data shown from the senses. The other notion of experience demands a verification which is really a consciousness-raising operation: it is an adversion to, e.g., one's own feelings, attitudes, moods and bodily movements. Non-sensuous perception supercedes and precedes sense perception.

> . . . we find that the final appeal to our experience is an appeal not so much to what we may verify through our senses as to what we may validate as meaningful to the experience of the self as an authentic self, to what phenomenologists call our "lived experience."[33]

This special "perception" of self and world is not limited to sense but instead includes our antecedent experience as a being-in-the-world: a primitive awareness of self and its world, of individual being in relation. This lived experience, this experience of self, provides the fundamental referent of revisionist theology.[34]

The experience of the individual in relation surfaces the final and grounding gift of basic faith. As one probes this lived experience of self, he discovers that not only does it yield a distinct notion of that self, and of the others that are its world, but beyond both of these there emerges a sense of the whole in which they are all one. Just as we become aware of our own existence in the process of relating to others, so we and others are differentiated by relation to a third presence.[35] "We are selves at all only because of our inalienable trust that our own existence and existence generally are somehow justified and made meaningful by the whole to which we know ourselves to belong."[36] As we experience our individual unity with a larger whole we gather strength to be a self--to exist at all--from the assurance that our lives are worthwhile. This sense of the value of reality, of the worth of existence for its own sake, is what allows us to continue and to embrace life and the world as meaningful. A sense of the being and value of life is a sense of an infinite whole in which we feel all are somehow included. This basic faith is a "sense of holiness" which supports human life and is thematized in the languages of religion and secularity as well.

And so for Tracy theology is faith seeking understanding. Our basic faith is given, it forces itself upon us, and it is not created by reason. But the attempt to display and understand it is a rational construction. The theologian can argue whether this ground is symbolized and conceptualized in an authentic manner, that is, in fidelity to our experience in a modern, empirical culture and in accord with the ethic of the community of scholars. Religion is not identical with basic faith but rather is one expression of it. The theologian questions not whether there is basic faith but how we can affirm its various expressions. Theology does not prove faith but demonstrates the adequacy and appropriateness of its encapsulation in religious belief. If this is the task of revisionist theology, basic faith is its assumption and not its conclusion. Basic faith, as basic, cannot and should not be proven. Yet it is the controlling idea of the whole project: the notion and possibility of investigation, correlation, and validation is based upon the supposition that there is a basic common faith behind various secular and religious expressions. This assumption allows the idea that both poles can be correlated and dictates that the philosophical tools selected must be those most useful in displaying this faith and in certifying its true expression. There would be no revisionism for Tracy without the keystone of basic faith.[37]

We have seen that the main worry of this theology is fidelity to our basic faith. This axiom of revisionism has been enlarged by the following qualifications: (1) The entire method is an appeal to experience. But this appeal to experience as the ground of meaning and truth is not ordinary. (2) The experience at issue is a faith in the value of our secular lives. It is an extraordinary but (paradoxically) typical confidence that our world and being are worthwhile. (3) The source of this sense of worth transcends self and yet includes it; it is transcendent and immanent. It is a relation to the whole which emerges within the experiential pattern of the self. Within the experience of self there emerges this major referent of Tracy's search for meaning and truth, viz., basic faith or a sense of the whole.[38] (4) It is the experience of the self as a self which contains this sense of worth and so is the proximate referent of theological statement. But the experience of self and whole is not limited to the usual philosophical fascination with sense perception. On the contrary, the experience of self is seen to be prior to sense perception. It is non-sensuous and vague, not sensual and discrete. It is an imprecise experience which grounds sense data rather than being grounded by them. (5) The formulation of this faith in language is the initial focus and the theological entry to this experience.

Under all of life is an experience of the importance and reality of the self and the world. By Tracy's definition, this is an experience of totality, it is ultimate and gracious and may be called religious. The religious function of all language would then be to re-present, either symbolically or in a self-conscious conceptuality, this confidence in the transcendental worth of us and our world. On Tracy's analysis of our secular and religious language, confidence in the worthwhileness of existence is constitutive of human experience as such and implies a referent that is necessary and so can be called "God."

Tracy's empirical appeal to basic faith as a criterion for meaning and truth includes an appeal to language. If basic faith is the first principle of his revisionism, the relationship between it and language is the second.

The Expression and Disclosure of Limit Faith

The pluralism and secularity of our modern theological context lead Tracy to eschew the search for any single, all-encompassing definition of religion. The scientific study of religion presents us with a multiplicity of practiced religions and a swarm of competing views on the "essence" of religion. In light of this conflicting pluralism, the formulation of a simple specific definition of religion acceptable to all is scarcely a possibilty. Furthermore, such a classicist tendency to metaphysical prescription is simply out of place in our non-classical, empiricist culture. But what Tracy does see as possible is the description of certain factors which mark what we call religious from that which we call moral, aesthetic, scientific, or political.[39] He insists that this procedure is not a quest for the determining core of all religion, but a taking note of certain (not all) relatively more superficial characteristics which seem to accompany whatever it is we mean by religion.

Tracy finds that one peculiar characteristic which marks the religious dimension in any language or experience is limit. A note of limit is present in that experience or language which we usually deem religious. This observation is the result of an empirical examination in the tradition of Ramsey and Ferre.[40] Drawing on their work, Tracy finds that the particular "logical character" of a religious dimension and language is that of limit. It brings us up against the edges of our words and our world. This is true of both explicitly religious texts and of whatever religious elements might be implicit in ordinary secular experience.

> My contention will be that all significant explicitly religious language and experience (the "religions") and all significant implicitly religious characteristics of our common experience (the "religious dimension") will bear at least the "family resemblance" of articulating or implying a limit-experience, a limit-language, or a limit-dimension.[41]

Thus to locate a limit dimension in any phenomenon is to locate a religious dimension therein. One finds the common point in secular experience and traditional religions by locating limit expressions in each and by inferring from them their common ground in a limit experience.

Basic faith is thus aptly named a limit faith and the language of its expression a limit language. The religious dimension is a faith "at" and "of" the limits and hence a faith properly called limit faith, limit-experience, or limit dimension. This limit faith takes expression in a concomitant limit language. The limit feature of our experienced religious dimension and its language is manifest as either a limit to our ordinary experience or the limit of that experience. Religious language, for Tracy, is disclosive language; it is a limit-language which discloses certain authentic limit experiences ("limits-to" our life and projects) and their foundational limit faith ("limits-of" our lives and projects). In other words, the manifestation of limit is expressive and disclosive: it expresses the limits of our being-in-the-world (finitude, contingency) and discloses the limit--the ground--of that same self (trust in the worth of human life and world) as well. Furthermore, the former often discloses the latter: as we meet limits to our being, the worth and possibility of living and doing are challenged and yet we find that we do go on, that we are assured of our worth by the very ground of our being. Human life in the face of contingency and finitude is made possible by the unconditional worthwhileness we experience at the edges of life. A convenient handle and a useful philosophical control for this is found in the concept of limit and in the association of this concept with the language and experience which we properly call religious.

The concept of limit becomes the key to the question of religious meaningfulness. "A particular experience or language is 'meaningful' when it discloses an authentic dimension of our experience as selves."[42] Meaningful (genuinely disclosive) expressions may be aesthetic, economic, political, etc. But do they bear that limit-character which would logically allow one to apply the term "religious" to them? When are language and experience religiously meaningful? Tracy sets one task of philosophical-hermeneutical investigation as the display of the "logical status" of certain language and experience. Does it have the religious note of a logical limit-character? Meaningfulness is the adequate thematization of human experience. Inasmuch as a phenomenological analysis of the language and experience involved shows the presence of limit, Tracy is prepared to argue that it is meaningful to refer to that language and experience as religious. The meaningfulness of the word "religious" is shown by attending to the language of limit and the experience of limit it names. To sum up: A (basically religious) limit-of faith emerges, among other places, in the (basically religious) experience of limits-to our being and is expressed in limit-language. The keynote of the religious is limit. Calling a phenomenon religious is justified if it can be shown to contain this peculiar religious sort of limit logic. Our originating faith, the experience in which it comes to us, and the language within which it is formulated are all linked by their participation in the markedly religious concept of limit.

There is a religious horizon to be found in common human experience. Limit questions and situations present themselves at the boundary of actual science, morality, and daily living. These questions and situations are not part of the normal internal matters of how to carry on specific scientific procedures, or the resolution of a moral dilemma within one's system, or the day-to-day ordering of life. At a certain point, one becomes concerned not about working the theorem, but about the possible grounds for any objective inquiry; not about the justification of some act in a moral system, but the justification for having any morality at all; not merely about how to go on, but why to bother. These are not questions about a science but about the quest for intelligibility, truth and value which drives the scientific enterprise.[43] These are questions about whether there is any ground which makes morality matter.[44] Such questions come from a point just outside the discipline itself where the practitioner asks not how to carry on his business but why it can even be carried on.

It is basic faith which reassures us when we peek over the edges of our structured, ordered, and balanced universe. This faith is the experience of a transcendental, benign whole with which we are one and with which we can measure our harmony. Anxiety over why science and morality can even be (limit-to) is assuaged by the disclosure that they are hooked into the basic faith which lies at the bottom of all (limit-of). There are limits to scientific inquiry (the inability of science to prove its presupposition that the universe is fundamentally intelligible, the presupposition that judgment about truth can be made, and the supposition that inquiry is valuable). There are limits to moral questioning (the inability to give moral reasons for being moral). It is along this frontier that we experience a "prior domain of existential fundamental reassurance and confidence in the worthwhileness and intelligibility of our existence."[45]

The same picture of the human person up against her limits emerges in situations of our everyday world. Among the fundamental and most challenging experiences of humankind are those of one's own finitude, e.g., error, sickness, guilt, sin, and the chilling quintessential limit, death. These instances shake our comfortable faith in ourselves and our world and make us question the totality of life; we become outsiders to our own world and begin to take its measure. They compel us to accept that the root horizon of our life is not one of our own making or within our own control: our lives are not completely ours. But this experience of finitude and anxiety is not the end. There is also present an experience of the transcendence of our limits, the ecstatic experience of joy or love or creation. These too push us from our ordinary view of our world and ourselves and take us beyond to a position from where we must view their limits. Such peak experiences are not an act of will but are givens, gifts that signal the transcendent basic faith grounding and allowing life and calming our anxiety. They put us in touch with the foundational, trustworthy meaning of our lives, the gracious horizon surrounding all that is human. Both the threatening situations of finitude and death (limits-to) and the peak experiences of love and joy (limits-of) are limits which come to us in our everyday life and yet move us to see the extraordinary. They take us to the edge of our world and there reveal the religious horizon of our world and lives.[46]

There are, then, strictly secular experiences which disclose a religious dimension or horizon to our lives. An analysis of science, morality, and the everyday reveals an experience of No-thing, an experience of limits.[47] Limit questions and limit situations disclose the reality of a dimension to our lives which is not usual.

> . . . a dimension which. . . discloses a reality . . . which functions as a final, now gracious, now frightening, now trustworthy, now absurd, always uncontrollable limit-of the very meaning of existence itself.[48]

This unusual, uncontrollable reality is commonly called religious. A major mark of its presence is the limit character of all its manifestations.

According to Tracy, when we use the word "religion" we use language to represent certain limit answers to certain limit questions. Religious language discloses a religious experience of basic limit trust. Though this trust may have been threatened in a boundary situation or by reflection upon limit questions of morality or science, it finds reaffirmation in religious language. This language of its nature brings a reassertion of our basic faith. Religious language is language which discloses a mode-of-being-in-the-world, a limit trust, a common and basic faith. This reassurance is not accomplished by science, morality, or culture (though it grounds them) but is the duty of religion. Religious language is a re-presentation of an already present confidence. Religion gives us the symbolic and linguistic forms through which faith can be reaffirmed on the level of self-conscious belief.[49] Our odd limit experiences demand an odd sort of language as well.

It is this conception of the relation between language and life-experience which sets Tracy's criteria for the meaningfulness of religious language in secular culture. The highlighting of limit experiences within our common human experience provides the empirical confirmation of the claim that secular experience has a dimension that can be characterized as religious. Inasmuch as it does re-present its own final horizon, secular language, thought, and activity have a religious dimension. The meaningfulness of religious language and experience can be tied to undeniable secular experiences and need not depend soley upon private, special and explicitly religious revelations. Whether it shows itself in explicitly religious language and experience or is implicit in common human experience, the thematization of our experience of being-in-the-world is properly called religious. Tracy claims that it is meaningful to apply the word "religious" to our secular world because we find there the limit-to and limit-of expressions and experiences which characterize the religious. From the strictly secular point of view, religious (limit) language is meaningful because the strictly secular provides appropriate existential referents.

The relationship between basic faith and limit language is also evidenced in Tracy's analysis of explicitly religious language. Having shown that the secular can be said to have a dimension adequately thematized as religious, he must now show that this same understanding of the religious is appropriate to the explicitly religious texts. Explicitly religious language should manifest the type of concern with limit which Tracy's investigation of common human experience claimed as uniquely religious. The same supposedly religious elements found in secularity must be present in the Christian tradition.

For proof of the limit character of the New Testament texts, Tracy relies upon Paul Ricoeur's philosophical elaboration of the metaphorical and structural operation of religious language and the concomitant development of structural criticism by contemporary exegetes.[50] According to this school of criticism, the foci of exegesis are located in the sense (language forms) and referent (the mode-of-being-in-the-world there presented) which structure the language. There is a special logical and a special experiential character. Tracy finds that both the sense and the referent of New Testament language reflect the odd limit character which marks the religious.

The New Testament uses of proverbs, eschatological sayings, and parables supports this view. New Testament language is limit language because the New Testament consistently breaks the traditional forms of expression it uses. By pushing the sense of these forms beyond their conventional boundary, the traditional literary vehicles are made to bear distinctly unusual burdens. The lingistic and historical explanation for Biblical language breaking its forms in order to communicate is too complex to be explained here.[51] However, it can be noted that the general pattern is that of metaphor--stretching the literal and usual into new shapes, bursting the genre's ordinary rules of sense and so communicating and engaging a new world. Thus the proverbs of Jesus are not the typical aphoristic wisdom literature they resemble, but rather they strain with paradox and hyperbole to undermine the typical assumptions of this language and life. For example, "Whoever seeks to gain his life will lose it, but whoever loses his life will preserve it" (Lk. 17:33; cf. Mk. 8:35) is not a sagacious bit of folklore as much as a shocking statement that what we expect--what we have learned to expect from common sense and the correct use of the genre--to be the case is not.[52] The same confounding of ordinary modes of wisdom appears in Jesus' proclamatory sayings. "The kingdom of God is not coming with signs to be observed; nor will they say, 'Lo, here it is!' or 'there!' for behold, the kingdom of God is in the midst of you." While such statements fall best into the genre of apocalyptic, they actually twist the typical apocalyptic expectations about the temporal and local coming of the kingdom and turn us back to our own world and present time. Structurally, the eschatological sayings of Jesus do not give the devotee of apocalyptic what she expects; the form is operating differently than is normal. It plays on the genre, moves beyond the rules for the genre's proper use, and yet its creative limit-use remains enough in accord with the relevant linguistic rules that communication does take place. The intensification of ordinary proverbial language and the overturning of chronological time in the eschatological proclamation sayings of the New Testament provide solid linguistic reasons for describing New Testament language as limit-language. This "going the limits" of the language is the result of crossing the expectation of a hearer who is familiar with the ordinary usage of the form.

The parables of Jesus are another good example of limit-language: they stretch linguistic rules to their limits; they shake us up by taking us to the edge of our world and language. By crossing two theoretical structures, the structure of the hearer's expectation and the structure of the speaker's actual expression, they sow dissonance where once there was harmony and break open a new world of possibilities for us. The structure of the parable acts to reorient us to the ultimate and extraordinary by disorienting the ordinary. So in the much discussed parable of the Good Samaritan (the non-redactional core is Lk. 10:30-35) we expect the Priest and the levite, as religious leaders and examples, to aid their fellow Jew in the ditch. We expect the Samaritan heretic to be irreligious and so to render no aid. But we are surprised.³⁵ The world is not as it seems. In such stories of everyday life, the extraordinary comes to us as our comfortable and controlled world is turned on its head. The parables are narrative elaborations of some basic metaphor formulated in such a way as to confront us with the limits-of our world. The point of the parables is in their sense, not in some allegory or moral application. This sense is a structural surprise which bears the hearer of the story to his limits and discloses an experience beyond the everyday.

The limit (religious) sense which breaks the ordinary forms of a language and pushes it to its limits is accompanied by the consequent revelation of a limit reference. The parables, proverbs, and sayings of Jesus redescribe our ordinary lives so as to give us a glimpse of new and extraordinary possibilities for being-in-the-world. They tell us that it is possible to live a life marked by response to an immanent other, a life marked by basic faith. Basic faith is the referent of this Biblical language.

> . . . "the religions" themselves, I believe, fundamentally ask us to allow the limit-experience of trust and confidence in the final graciousness of reality itself to provide the basic orientation of

our lives.[54]

The limit sense of Biblical language belies a limit reference: the New Testament's breaking of genre displays the limit-to human being and brings us face to face with the limit-of human being. The religious use of language drives ordinary language forms like proverbs, sayings and parables to their limits and in the process reveals the foundation of ordinary life. This language shows us that authentic existence requires that we live at our limits, which is to say conscious of our basic faith in secularity, in a new awareness of that "other," that whole, with which we are one. For Tracy, both the sense and the referent of explicitly religious language have a limit character.

When language is put to religious use, whether in Christian tradition or our common human experience, it always becomes limit language. Such language thematizes a phenomenon which is both strictly secular and explicitly religious, namely, the basic faith grounding human activity. The religious language and experience of the New Testament re-present our (always threatened) basic confidence in existence as the fundamental mode of our being-in-the-world; they reassure us that the final reality of our lives is trustworthy. The same experience comes to us in the questions and situations of our common human experience. The phrase "religious dimension" (and its equivalents) is correctly applied when it can be seen to refer to limit experience. These experiences arise in context both of limits-to and limits-of our secular lives: "The religious dimension is most clearly recognized in such limit experiences as (negatively) anxiety or (positively) fundamental trust in the very worthwhileness of our existence."[55] Both common secular experience and uncommon Christian metaphors and metaphorical elaborations bring us to awareness of our limits, to the real context and texture of our lives, to basic faith and its origins. The referent of explicitly religious language is the same experience of the whole which comes to us in the religious aspects of our common human experience.

Revisionist theology is a response to comtemporary challenges to the existential and conceptual meaningfulness of religion. These challenges are met by a fundamental theological inquiry into the criteria for meaning and truth. The limit expressions and limit experiences disclosed in common human experience and religious texts are the key. Tracy's discussion of meaning, meaningfulness, and truth assumes the presence of basic faith and its disclosure in limit expressions and limit situations.

This view of religious language and experience is Tracy's reply to the accusation that religion is existentially vacuous. He argues that meaningfulness is a matter of locating a referent in experience. Tracy is convinced that the presence of a certain sort of language betokens the presence of a certain sort of experience and vice versa.[56] Religious language must be linked to religious experience. When it is, it is meaningful. Being religious is signaled by having the logical character of limit. Religious language is always (though not only) a language of limit and its underlying referent is our basic limit faith, a trusting mode-of-being-in-the-world. Tracy finds that religion is woven into the fabric of our lives.

But there is also the question of truth. Even though basic faith may be disclosed by philosophical analysis, there remains the further question of the conditions for the possibility of that faith. What is it that makes possible the trust we experience in our selves? Why do we experience the worth of human life and its world? An attempt to provide a reflective account of this religious experience requires an inference to the ground or origin of this experience.[57]

Metaphysics asks about the adequacy of the conceptual "handle" for whatever is the ultimate condition of our experience. This is a quest for a reflective understanding of the existential faith constitutive of all human existence, an understanding "wherein existential faith can be represented in an express, thematic, and conceptually precise way."[58] An adequate conception of this referent must be true, that is, it must meet the two general criteria of metaphysics: (1) Is the formulation internally coherent? (2) Is it an adequate and accurate grasp of our experience?[59] The workings of transcendental and metaphysical thought are governed by Tracy's conception of basic faith. Recall that for Tracy the most accurate explanation of our experience and the referent of all that is religious and therefore ultimate, is the experience of self as a self and the basic faith and sense of the whole which comes to us therein. This is the level of experience suitable to a transcendental investigation and as the control on any metaphysical thematizing.

Is there a limit-concept which captures the basic faith behind the limit language and experience found in common human experience and Christian texts? Concretely, this question of conceiving the objective referent for religion is the question of God. Does theism provide the best reflective articulation of the objective basis for the limit language and experience which compose theology's two sources? Tracy believes that the secular philosopher and the theologian can agree that it does.[60] The objective ground for our secular/religious faith can be conceptualized as theistic. Religion requires the "reality dimension" brought by theism; if there is no objective referent behind religious experience then that experience is an interesting psychological occurrence but hardly cognitive, hardly integrated into all that we know as real. But the religious claims to be the ground of all that we know and do. As such, its referent must be necessary by definition; whatever grounds all that is real must itself be real.[61] Theism is the best articulation of such a referent.[62]

> . . . only an affirmation of the reality of God as the one necessary existent can validate our very understanding of our selves as selves, our primordial and unconquerable basic faith in the ultimate worthwhileness of our existence.[63]

Whatever it is about our experience of the whole that justifies our trust in the worth of life, that alone is properly named "God." Tracy echoes Ogden's conviction that "the primary use or function of 'God' is to refer to the objective ground in reality itself of our ineradicable confidence in the final worth of our existence."[64] Bluntly, if there is "religious" experience there must be "God." God is the conceptualization for what makes possible that faith experience which allows all human knowing and doing.

For David Tracy, then, the first move in the search for meaningfulness and truth is a look to experience. In the matter of meaningfulness, he looks to the carriers of this basic faith (experience, symbol, myth, mediating experiences) and constructs a demonstration that they do indeed draw their life from that limit faith. As Tracy turns to the problem of truth his concern becomes more conceptual than existential. Claims of truth for a conceptualization demand internal coherence, adequacy to the experience being explained, and appropriateness to Christian tradition.[65] In order to validate the theistic conception, after checking for coherence and congruence with tradition, Tracy looks to the most fundamental experience at hand as the guarantor of truth. Not only do we experience basic trust, but our faith experience is further differentiated as a participation in some sort of whole. The question of the reality of this whole and of our relationship to it is the question of the "objective" reality of the faith experience it generates. Metaphysics is an attempt to validate our common human experience by explaining ontologically why it is our common human experience.

> . . . the constitutive principle of the process tradition insists that philosophers note their experience as experiencing selves rather than their sense-perception of objects as the fundamental experiential and, <u>thereby</u>, metaphysical ground of all their basic concepts.[66]

The matter may be conceptual and cognitive but the proof is still pre-eminently existential. Metaphysical truth is the demonstration of the experiential link between the transcendental conceptual expression of the religious (theism) and its originating referent. Tracy consistently equates meaningfulness with the existential, with the appeal to experience; word and experience are somehow hooked together. If meaningfulness is a tie between experience and language, especially between certain experiences and the term "religious," truth is the marking of the same tie between a certain experience and the term "God." Criteria for truth do not totally collapse into those for meaningfulness. After all, they do have different concerns. The latter is more experiential, the former more conceptual. But both attend to basic faith and look primarily to experience.

Basic faith is the limit faith expressed in limit experiences and limit language. A phenomenology can disclose this "religious" faith and thereby publicly establish the existential meaningfulness of religious discourse. A metaphysics can publicly validate this experience as conceptually true. Thus the representation of limit faith in limit expressions is an essential feature of Tracy's revisionist foundations. It allows for a public discourse. It allows for a genuine reciprocity of critique by theology's two sources. It provides the structure and possibility of revisionist investigation, correlation, and validation.

A Public Theology

The complexity of Tracy's revisionism makes it dangerous to reduce it to a handy summary. Nevertheless, if one took up only the thread of method and presumed the context and above, several points might safely be highlighted: (1) Theology must be justified as a public inquiry. That is, its criteria and arguments must be accessible and acceptable to the community of scholars. Tracy's project is a search for such a theological foundation. (2) In response, Tracy posits two general and related criteriological categories: adequacy to experience and appropriateness to Christian tradition. Both call upon the finest historical, philosophical and literary tools available. They echo his belief that Christian theology must be accountable to the general experience of humankind as well as to the specific experience of the Christian community. Each of these poles may criticize the other: the appropriate confronts the adequate and the adequate may question what is appropriate. In point of fact a fundamental theologian must pay special attention to the category of adequacy. For the explicitly religious pole must be tested by philosophical criteria of adequacy. What are the experiential criteria to which theological statements must be adequate? This question assures the public nature and credibility of the enterprise. (3) In the end, all relevant criteria are really varying forms of adequacy to our non-sensuous experience of the self as a self. More specifically, reference is to the experience of basic faith which is found there and to the vague originating experience of the whole. This type of experience is our most ultimate; it is the ground which supports and allows all meaningful human activity. (4) Tracy defines this as "religious." The experience of the self as a self discloses the basic faith and the sense of the whole which constitute religious experience and language. Tracy insists that the religious is consistently conjoined with the logical character of limit. Basic faith experience is experience of limit in our lives; it is an experience of limit which comes to us in the experience of limits-to and limits-of our world. Language (or a situation) is used religiously (and truly) when it represents our already present limit trust. (5) Three modes of adequacy to this basically religious limit faith are proposed as criteria for all theological statements: meaning, meaningfulness, and truth. Meaning is simply the superficial adequacy of consistency and coherence; it is a logical mapping which uncovers and charts the limit character of what is called religious. The experientially meaningful must be logically coherent as well. Meaningfulness is the adequacy of language and experience as an existential disclosure of the primal assurance that is our basic faith experience. Truth derives from our sense that there is a whole and we are part of it. Truth is the adequacy of conceptual language as a description and implication of the transcendental conditions for the possibility of our basic trust.[67] To have meaningfulness and to have truth is to offer an accurate grasp of our most basic experience. (6) The inquiry known as fundamental theology is structured by an ordered concern with these modes of adequacy. The investigative moment is a hermeneutic-phenomenological look to the meaning and meaningfulness of both the Biblical witness and secular experience. The moment of correlation notes that with respect to their origin in basic faith both theological sources are identical. Thus they can be correlated, they can confirm and check each other. There is no contradiction between the secular and the religious as both reflect in their own way the same ground. Validation is the final moment. It looks to the truth of the meaningful, i.e., to the conception of that object in reality (the whole we experience in the self as having positive ontological status) to which the religious refers. Revisionism then is an experience-oriented investigation into the meaningfulness of religious experience and language, a logical investigation of its meaning, and a transcendental investigation into its truth. All of these moments of Tracy's revisionism derive from his axiomatic insistence on the ultimacy of the basic faith dimension, its link with certain other experience and language, and the recognition of this as a description of religion.

David Tracy's <u>Blessed Rage for Order</u> suggests the key issues for a contemporary foundational theology and presents a concrete plan for responding to them. Let us now take a longer view: what sort of theology is it which Tracy sees as meeting his revisionist requirements? Most of all, it will be a public discourse. This goal will manifest itself in the development of a methodological, empirical and linguistic foundation for inquiry. This theology is fundamental precisely because it is methodological. It wants to set the various terms and relations which allow and direct any actual doing of theology. It insists that each theologian "must attempt to articulate and defend an explicit method of inquiry, and use that method to interpret the symbols and texts of our common life and of Christianity."[68] It is empirical. The public and methodological exigence translates into the problem of measuring the appropriateness and adequacy of theology's two sources against the basic experience they thematize. This is a demand for the setting of criteria. It is linguistic. The basic criteria in theological discourse are those for meaning and truth. Tracy's concerns are methodological in that he seeks his foundation in the criteria for carrying on theological discourse. His concerns are empirical and linguistic because the methodological quest is dominated by a referral to the experience disclosed and captured in language.[69] Tracy sets himself a heuristic for drafting a theology that is methodologically self-conscious, empirically oriented, and linguistically focused. In this way theology is to become public and credible.

David Tracy's own version of the dialogical theology he calls for relates fides and ratio in a reciprocal critique which takes the form of a public investigation, correlation, and validation of common experience and religious texts as properly religious and theistic. In this way, one discloses a foundation for theological discourse and a source of academic credibility. Since this theology revolves around the problems of meaning and truth, it will naturally seek its foundations in the criteria for meaning and truth. For Tracy this fundament is the ineluctable experience of basic faith which is revealed through language and other penultimate experiences of human thought and life. But this is only one possible approach to the issues. One can accept the issues raised by Tracy without finally embracing Tracy's own plan for dealing with them. There are other possibilities.

One must distinguish the issues and parameters of the investigation from the solutions offered by various particular methods. There is room to put the question of whether Tracy has satisfactorily concluded the search for foundations which he calls for. Are we at rock-bottom with his appeal to experience or not? There seems to be no reason to disagree with Tracy's insistence that contemporary fundamental theology should look to method, language, and the empirical in formulating a theology that is available for our secular and pluralist world. But there are many ways to fill this prescription. If we agree that a major issue of fundamental theology is criteria for meaning and truth, are we further compelled to accept the methods of phenomenology and metaphysics which Tracy proposes for dealing with this issue? Are there other options? Has David Tracy really located the foundations of theology? More important, is the search for foundations itself wrong-headed?

It may be that Tracy is so busy plying a method for the revelation of experience that--contrary to appearances--he overlooks the method of attention to language. It may be that whatever "foundations" are available for theology lie in this new direction. Specifically, Wittgenstein's version of the linguistic turn may supply additional methodological sophistication to revisionist method. Attention to this perspective may bring new clarity to theological inquiry.

Notes

1. <u>BRO</u>, is concerned to outline a program for fundamental or foundational theology. A systematics is another matter. Its direction is put forth in Tracy, "Modes of Theological Argument," <u>Theology Today</u> 32 (January 1977): 387-95. Tracy's systematic theology is fully outlined in Tracy, <u>The Analogical Imagination</u> (New York: Crossroad Publishing Co., 1981). While he does refine some of his earlier positions in <u>Analogical</u>, his foundations remain.

2. <u>BRO</u>, p. 5-7.

3. <u>BRO</u>, p. 9.

4. <u>BRO</u>, p. 4. ". . . the theologian <u>qua</u> theologian is committed to explicating the meaning and truth of the answers provided by the text to the 'fundamental questions' of human existence." <u>BRO</u>, p. 61, n. 44.

5. <u>BRO</u>, p. 43.

6. <u>BRO</u>, p. 45.

7. <u>BRO</u>, pp. 43-45. This idea of requiring criteria for appropriateness and criteria for adequacy is drawn from Ogden, "What is Theology?," pp. 25-27, 30-34.

8. Tillich, Bultmann, and neo-orthodoxy in general are good examples of this false correlation which overlooks the value of secular answers and ignores the reality of religious doubts and questions. Cf. <u>BRO</u>, pp. 45-46.

9. <u>BRO</u>, p. 47.

10. <u>BRO</u>, p. 49.

11. The view of meaning as a function of the unity of sense and referent reflects an important supposition of Tracy's project. He sketches his use of "sense" and "referent" in <u>BRO</u>, p. 51: "The 'sense' of the text means the internal structure and meaning of the text as that structure can be determined through the ordinary methods of semantic and literary-critical inquiries. The 'referents' of the text do not pertain to the meaning 'behind' the text (e.g., the author's <u>real</u> intention or the social-cultural situation of the text). Rather, to shift metaphors, 'referent' basically manifests the meaning 'in front of' the text, i.e., that way of perceiving reality, that mode of being-in-the-world which the text opens up for the intelligent reader."

12. <u>BRO</u>, p. 55. This conjunction of basic faith and the meaning of

meaningfulness is a major theme.

13. BRO, p. 52.

14. BRO, p. 67.

15. BRO, p. 55. If this is the foundation of all, it is also open and available to all, i.e., public. ". . . if transcendental reflection does mediate the conditions of the possibility of experience as such, there is no 'special' particular experience or set of experiences that one can appeal to for 'verifying' or 'falsifying' that mediation." BRO, p. 63, n. 64.

16. This is a post-critical reinterpretation of Kant's transcendental project. Kant's fixation on the centrality of reason is replaced by the presumption of the centrality of an originating lived experience. Clear and distinct undestandings are derived from a comprehensive, vague and primordial experience. For a good summary of the development of this new notion of the transcendental task of metaphysics by a thinker who has influenced Tracy's position see Emerich Coreth, Metaphysics, with a critique by Bernard J. F. Lonergan, trans. Joseph Donceel (New York: Herder and Herder, 1968), pp. 17-44. Cf. BRO, pp. 67-68.

17. BRO, p. 56.

18. BRO, pp. 54-55.

19. This conception of meaningfulness (and not just truth) as a function of mediation is clearly stated in BRO, chapter four: "At such moments, we seek aid for understanding, for raising to explicit concsciousness--in a word, for mediating--the immediacy of that experience by our own powers of intelligent and critical introspection." BRO, p. 66. "Second, all these modes of analysis can be generically labeled 'phenomenological' in the broad sense of mediating the relationship of particular expressions either linguistic (e.g., metaphors or concepts) or non-linguistic (e.g., images) to our immediate lived experience. Third, whenever and however such mediation occurs, the particular symbol, image, metaphor, myth or concept is rendered meaningful to various degrees of adequacy dependent upon its disclosive power for our lived experience." BRO, p. 69.

20. "The analysis of 'common human experience and language,' therefore, should include philosophical reflection of the phenomenological-transcendental type and should theryby demand the application of all three sets of criteria: 'meaningfulness,' 'meaning,' and 'truth.' A particular experience or language is 'meaningful' when it discloses an authentic dimension of our experience as selves. It has 'meaning' when its cognitive claims can be expressed conceptually with internal coherence. It is 'true' when transcendental or metaphysical analysis shows its 'adequacy to experience' by explicating how a

particular concept (e.g., time, space, self, or God) functions as a fundamental 'belief' or 'condition of possibility' of all our experience." BRO, p. 71.

21. Tracy moves through a progressive specificity of and maintains a continual anchoring in common human experience: our common experience can be validly seen as religious, the religious dimension is best thematized as theistic, and the Christological expression of theistic religion is the most adequate.

22. BRO, p. 8.

23. BRO, p. 16, n. 13. One sees the same schema in Ogden's distinction between existential and reflective faith. Existential faith is that faith constitutive of human existence. It is the self-conscious acceptance of and adjustment to life which is peculiar to being human. Reflective faith is the re-presentation of existential faith in a coherent conceptuality. Ogden, "The Task of Philosophical Theology," in The Future of Philosophical Theology ed. Robert A. Evans (Philadelphia: Westminster Press, 1971) pp. 55-84. Cf. BRO, p. 153.

24. Clearly, such a move leaves one open to the objection that the revisionist attitude is not a function of the disclosure of experiences but rather is created by definition and presuppositions.

25. In order to put this claim in context, recall that the intended audience fro BRO is the contemporary American academic community. In an intellectually differentiated group there will be intellectual controls on the mediation of religion and culture. Any intellectual problems with this mediation are likely to have existential import.

26. BRO, p. 8. This faith is secular because it is the common faith grounding those who are fully secular and non-religious and because it is a faith in this world, in the extraordinary value of ordinary life.

27. Ogden, "Theology and Religious Studies," p. 7. Tracy admits (for example in BRO, p. 19, n. 46 and p. 116, n. 58) that this conception of basic faith is inspired by Ogden. Schubert Ogden is often a source for Tracy. Since Ogden's treatment is sometimes more developed or more clearly put than Tracy's, I will not hesitate to refer to it for clarification.

28. Ogden, "Theology and Religious Studies," pp. 7-8; Ogden, "Task," pp. 56-57; Ogden, The Reality of God (New York: Harper & Row, 1966), pp. 27-45; Tracy, BRO, pp. 102-09.

29. Alfred North Whitehead, Process and Reality: An Essay in Cosmolgy (New York: Macmillan Press, 1929), p. 246, quoted in Ogden, "Present Prospects for Empirical Theology," in Bernard E. Meland, ed.,

The Future of Empirical Theology, Essays in Divinity, vol. 7 (Chicago: University of Chicago Press, 1969), p. 82.

30. Whitehead, Modes of Thought (New York: Macmillan Press, 1938), pp. 148-49, quoted in Ogden, "Prospects," p. 82.

31. BRO, pp. 172-74, 191-92. For a good account of the "turn to the subject" which was also formative for Tracy see Lonergan, The Subject (Milwaukee: Marquette University Press, 1968).

32. Whitehead, Process and Reality, p. 252, quoted in BRO, p. 192, n. 7; BRO, p. 173.

33. BRO, p. 66.

34. BRO, pp. 64-66. Cf. Ogden, "Prospects," pp. 77-85.

35. Ogden, "Prospects," p. 85. See also the quotation there from Whitehead, Modes, p. 140: "Apart from this sense of transcendent worth, the otherness of reality would not enter into our consciousness. There must be value beyond ourselves. Otherwise everything experienced would be merely a barren detail in our solipisist mode of existence. . . ."

36. Ogden, "Theology and Religious Studies," p. 7.

37. "An explicit and full recognition of this faith as, in fact, the common faith shared by secularist and modern Christian is perhaps the most important insight needed to understand the contemporary theological situation in its full dimensions and its real possibilities." BRO, p. 8.

38. This experience of the self as a part of the whole also includes the experience of the self as an exemplar of that whole and is later developed into a neo-classical metaphysics. This follows the tenet that the experience of the universe is given in the experience of the self. Here is the ground of both the phenomenological search for meaning and the metaphysical search for truth.

39. Tracy simply claims to highlight certain "family resemblances" among that which we call religious. Contemporary theological speculation accomplishes this by taking either a functional approach, e.g., Peter L. Berger, The Sacred Canopy: Elements of a Sociological Theory of Religion (New York: Doubleday, 1967) or a substantive approach, e.g., Schleiermacher, Otto, Lonergan. Tracy pursues the substantive approach; he focuses on our limit experience as distinctive of the religious. Tracy, "Metaphor and Religion," pp. 93-94, and BRO, pp. 92-93. Whether or not Tracy's project is unwittingly essentialist is another matter.

40. BRO, pp. 120-24. Cf. Ian Ramsey, Religious Language: An Empirical Placing of Theological Phrases (New York: Macmillan Press,

1963); Frederick Ferré, "Mapping the Logic of Models in Science and Theology," in New Essays on Religious Language, ed. Dallas M. High (New York: Oxford University Press, 1969), pp. 54-97; Ferré, Language, Logic and God (New York: Harper & Row, 1961). Tracy also relies on other figures who take this type of linguistic analysis seriously, e.g., Ogden, Reality, pp. 25-40, and Ricoeur, "Specificity." The linguistic analysis of Ramsey and Ferré provides Tracy with logical reasons for his (more phenomenologically inspired) use of the terms "limit language" and "limit experience." They also support his contention that the religious language and experience which founds theological discourse must have an existential referent and be coherent.

41. BRO, p. 93.

42. BRO, p. 71. See BRO, pp. 64-71.

43. BRO, pp. 96-100, 113, n. 26. Cf. Lonergan, Method pp. 3-25, 101-05, and Lonergan, Insight, pp. 271-430. "Since these limit-questions legitimately follow from scientific inquiry itself, they are not imposed extrinsically upon scientists by 'religious' types but rather are well within the scientific inquirer's own horizon. . . .No inquirer can commit himself to the task of authentic self-transcendence (i.e., intelligent, rational, and responsible thought and action) and then deny his own need to seek the ultimate intelligent, rational and responsible grounds for such inquiry and action." BRO, p. 99. Although Tracy relies on Lonergan in this discussion, he is convinced that "other philosophical positions also mediate a recognition of a religious dimension or horizon of science. Either Louis Dupre's Hegelian phenomenology or Alfred North Whitehead's process philosophy or Stephen Toulmin's linguistic analysis of the 'limiting questions' in science all mediate a similar understanding." BRO, p. 99.

44. BRO, pp. 100-04; Ogden, Reality, pp. 27-43.

45. BRO, p. 99.

46. BRO, pp. 105-08.

47. BRO, p. 107. Cf. BRO, p. 118, n. 88.

48. BRO, p. 108.

49. BRO, p. 108. For development of this theme see Paul Ricoeur's work, beginning with The Symbolism of Evil, trans. Emerson Buchanan (Boston: Beacon Press, 1969), especially pp. 347-557, and Ricoeur, "The Problem of Double Meaning as Hermeneutic Problem and as Semantic Problem," trans. Kathleen McLaughlin, in Ricoeur, The Conflict of Interpretation: Essays in Hermeneutics, ed. Don Ihde (Evanston: Northwestern University Press, 1974), pp. 62-78.

50. Tracy relies especially on Paul Ricoeur, "Interpretation Theory," (University of Chicago: May, 1971, mimeographed). See the more accessible Paul Ricoeur, Interpretation Theory: Discourse and the Surplus of Meaning (Fort Worth: Texas Christian University Press, 1976), and his special issue of Semeia, especially Ricoeur, "The Specificity of Religious Language," Semeia 4 (1975): 107-48. Structuralists and literary exegetes of the sort favored by the journal Semeia are a main source for this position in biblical scholarship. For a sketch of its development and the major figures see Norman Perrin, Jesus and the Language of the Kingdom: Symbol and Metaphor in New Testament Interpretation (Philadelphia: Fortress Press, 1976) pp. 89-193.

51. BRO, pp. 124-31. For Tracy's sources in the literature see BRO, pp. 124 and 139, n. 28. Cf. Perrin, Jesus and the Language of the Kingdom, pp. 89-215 and Ricoeur, "Specificity."

52. The contrast here is between a proverb like "A stitch in time saves nine" which hardly discloses that whole which gives us meaning, and "Let the dead bury the dead" which is not a common sense bit of advice but a disconcerting disconnecting from the respectable and acceptable and the revelation of new directions for grief and life. BRO, p. 134.

53. John Dominic Crossan, "The Good Samaritan: Towards a Generic Definition of Parable," Semeia 2 (1974): 82-112; Crossan, The Dark Interval: Towards a Theology of Story (Niles, Illinois: Argus Communications, 1975) especially pp. 104-08.

54. BRO, p. 134.

55. Tracy, "Metaphor and Religion," p. 95.

56. Tracy insists on the tie between language and experience. For him, the sharpening of our language allows the experience behind it to come through more fully, while the sharpening of our attention to experience allows us to appreciate the accuracy and fruitfulness of our religious language. "The liberation of our language and the liberation of our experience go hand in hand." BRO, p. 133.

57. The project is an investigation and validation of theistic belief vis à vis the basic faith it re-presents. "Does theistic language adequately re-present the most basic faith presupposed by all our existing and understanding? Properly understood, that is the philosophical question of God. . . . Rather, religious language, indeed all religious expression, is used to represent the most basic belief (more exactly, that basic common human confidence and trust in existence) which underlies all our other basic beliefs (for example, the belief that it is ultimately meaningful to pursue a moral life). Religion, in short, is basically a representative phenomenon whose cognitive claims can be investigated only by a mode of reflection (metaphysics) whose task is precisely the investigation of all

claims to re-present our basic beliefs and the conditions of the possibility of all our existing and understanding." BRO, pp. 154-55.

58. BRO, p. 153,

59. BRO, p. 172.

60. "If, as we insisted above, the primary existential use for the word 'God' is to refer to the objective ground in reality itself for those limit-languages and limit-experiences of an ultimate worth of our existence, our commitment to the good, and our struggle to achieve it; if the primary logical need for explicating this reality is a coherent limit-concept, then, on secular grounds alone, one need not hesitate to articulate that existential faith in explicitly theistic terms." BRO, p. 183. Cf. BRO, p. 154.

61. See Tracy's positive discussion of Anselm's famous proof in BRO, pp. 185-87.

62. For Tracy, neo-classical theism is especially attractive. This is hardly surprising given his general reliance on process thought. "Neo-classical" refers here to the tradition of the philosophers A. N. Whitehead and Charles Hartshorne and the theologian John Cobb. Schubert Ogden's thought, upon which Tracy relies a good deal, is a modified version. Tracy elaborates his process theism in BRO, pp. 175-87.

63. BRO, p. 186. "More exactly, only the reality of God, itself reinterpreted in process metaphysical categories, can account for that original and ineluctable confidence in the worthwhileness of existence which the earlier analysis of the religious dimension of our common experience portrayed." BRO, p. 174.

64. Ogden, Reality, p. 37. Cf. BRO, p. 183.

65. This is a Christian version of the two criteria for metaphysics with which Tracy began his discussion (BRO, p. 172). For Tracy's elaboration of these three points as a standard and the ways in which process theism fulfills them see BRO, pp. 181-87.

66. BRO, p. 173 (emphasis mine). Note as well Tracy, "Theology as Public," p. 282: "In this case, only frankly metaphysical evidence will provide the experiential warrents and backings needed for Christian God-language." (Emphasis mine).

67. ". . .its 'meaningfulness' may be found in the existential disclosure (e.g., reassurance) which such situations and language allow. The 'truth' claims of such language will need the explicit raising of the question of God as the objective referent in reality for such experiences (cf. chapters seven and eight)." BRO, p. 118, n. 92.

68. BRO, p. 3.

69. This view is summed up in BRO, p. 135: "Religious language does not present a new, a supernatural world wherein we may escape the only world we know or wish to know. Rather that language re-presents our always threatened basic confidence and trust in the very meaningfulness of even our most cherished and most noble enterprises, science, morality, and culture. That language discloses the reassurance needed that the final reality of our lives is in fact trustworthy."

It should also be noted that other revisionists share this concern to develop a method and to attend to language and experience. For example, Ogden is clearly in the same camp as Tracy and has provided Tracy with many of his own positions. Langdon Gilkey is another influential revisionist whose project evidences these same general lines. For a comparison and contrast of Tracy and Gilkey see Ommen, "Verification in Theology: A Tension in the Revisionist Method," The Thomist 43 (July 1979): 357-84. The briefest introduction to these three revisionists is their reply to the mysteriously inadequate article on their work by Peter Berger, "Secular Theology and the Rejection of the Supernatural: Reflections on Recent Trends," Theological Studies 38 (March 1977): 39-56. See Langdon Gilkey, Schubert Ogden, and David Tracy, "Responses to Peter Berger," Theological Studies 39 (September, 1978): 486-507.

CHAPTER THREE
UNDERSTANDING THE WITTGENSTEINIAN PERSPECTIVE

On Reading Wittgenstein

There are few works of contemporary philosophy and philosophically inclined theology which do not at least mention Ludwig Wittgenstein. Certainly a good deal of the current philosophical and theological fondness for language has been generated by his work directly or by that of his pupils or detractors. Although there has been general acceptance of Wittgenstein's importance in stimulating the development of a major strain of philosophical inquiry, this historical concession has not been accompanied by an equally widespread appropriation of his actual philosophical method. In fact, paradoxically, the certainty concerning his historical and personal influence is matched by an uncertainty over the exact nature of his philosophical contribution. As is often the case with those who have claimed to shift the axis of the philosophical world, there remains a good bit of confusion and conflict over where and even whether Wittgenstein has succeeded in repositioning that axis.

The confusion over the "Wittgenstein shift" has naturally retarded the theological appropriation of that shift. Since Wittgenstein wrote virtually nothing for publication on the subject of religion, theology must, for the most part, infer the implications of his philosophy for its concerns.[1] Furthermore, there has been a slurring of the distinction between Wittgenstein's own thought and the various schools and thinkers influenced by it. The unique and original turn of Wittgenstein's thought and the great number and variety of those who claim his mantle make it difficult to agree on the shape of a properly Wittgensteinian theology. Was Wittgenstein a positivist whose views naturally generate the sort of non-cognitivist view of religion fashioned by a Braithwaite or a van Buren?[2] Or perhaps his thought supports the "fideism" suggested by a Winch or a Phillips?[3] Or it may be that, as someone like Jerry Gill would insist, there is no such thing as a truly Wittgensteinian fideism or a truly Wittgensteinian positivism.[4] There are also writers like David Burrell who prefer to gather many diverse views on religion and language under the Wittgensteinian umbrella of attentiveness to language, and so are not too helpful in separating the strands and locating a clear outline of Wittgenstein himself.[5] The portrait of Wittgenstein is somewhat of a jumble.

How is it that a man whose favorite authors included Kierkegaard, Dostoievsky, and Augustine came to be labled a positivist? How is it that someone who believed it counterproductive to present theses and theories in philosophy generates quarrels over his doctrines? How is it that a thinker who attacked the quest for a scientific philosophy as impossible and misplaced also inspires a book advocating a scientific philosophy of religion?[6] One thing is certain: arguments over Wittgenstein's relevance for the philosophical quest of the examined life or for the theological probing of <u>homo religiosus</u> reflect a basic uncertainty and confusion about what Ludwig Wittgenstein said and why he bothered. Thus the first step in any dialogue between Wittgenstein and theology is to be clear about which picture of Wittgenstein shall be operative. With which Wittgenstein are we to converse?

Much of the disagreement over the nature of the Wittgenstein shift arises from a conflict in hermeneutic. Wittgenstein was concerned with what is most fundamental in philosophy, viz., with method, with the framework for doing philosophy at all. But his later thought is a radical critique of his earlier thought and a radical reorientation of the problem of language and method. Furthermore, this mature work does not resemble traditional philosophical prose but rather seems to be an open set of organized puzzles and occasional conclusions. It is not surprising, then, that there has been some discussion about the appropriate approach to the interpretation of the later Wittgenstein. The major hermeneutic possibilities reduce to two: did he see his new perspective as the laying out of a new theory or was his method a useful exercise in consciousness-raising? Is clarity to be found in foundational doctrines or within a personal conversion to linguistic self-awareness? The latter hermeneutic appears to be the most fruitful. Wittgenstein was interested in developing a linguistic therapy for the linguistically begotten problems which bedevil philosophy. It will be the supposition of our theological dialogue that, especially in the later period, Wittgenstein should be read with a therapeutic rather than a dogmatic emphasis. The tendency to view philosophical problems as fundamentally theoretical is precisely what Ludwig Wittgenstein wished to curb. He was sure that this sickness is as common as it is radical. In fact, there is a tendency to overlook the therapeutic cast of Wittgenstein's own work and to misread it as the development of a new philosophical dogma. This is a mistake, philosophically and hermeneutically, but it is not a stupid mistake.

Ludwig Wittgenstein often expressed fear that his work would be misunderstood and distorted. At the conclusion of a term at Cambridge he is reported to have remarked: "The only seed that I am likely to sow is a certain jargon."[7] A review of the voluminous literature on Wittgenstein testifies to the validity of his fears. The parroting of derivative catch phrases such as "meaning is use" or "words have meaning only in their game" has almost obscured the stimulating and creative character of their origin. Papers on his "doctrine" of the "language-game" and attempts to sharpen his "hopelessly underdeveloped" notion of "form of life" abound. There is no shortage of books and monographs purporting to systematize for him his "philosophy of language" or to draw out his supposed metaphysics.[8] But such efforts to better control and better formulate Wittgentein's doctrine are misdirected. Not only do they distort Wittgenstein's intent, they are the antithesis of it. It is not only in theology that a fascination with dogma can be lethal to the searching mind, for concern with doctrine has a tendency to distract one from the methodological nature of the Wittgensteinian shift. This distraction accounts for the two conflicting viewpoints behind the various interpretations of his corpus. It obscures the fact that the point of his investigation is to make us not disciples but better thinkers. Wittgenstein's contribution lies in his method: He shows us a whole new way of seeing philosophical problems. The concepts he actually uses are merely tools in a particular discussion--a discussion taken up in order to effect a change in the reader's vision. Jargon, theoretical problems, and systems are not the crux of Wittgenstein's own linguistic philosophy but are the cause and occasion for displaying its new procedure.

Wittgenstein's aim was therapeutic, not theoretic. The key to reading especially his later work is to note where he goes for answers and what that shows us about the nature of our puzzles and the shape of our task. It is a new way of looking at philosophical problems; it is not a new set of positions that is important but a new way of viewing the puzzles. More specifically, his work provides a set of exercises designed to help the reader discover the linguistic roots of his or her own philosophical thinking. This discovery is not the end of philosophy, but the beginning; it does not answer problems, but dissolves pseudo-problems and clarifies what remains; it is a radical, methodological move, not the proposition of yet another system. Failure to recognize this explains the conflicting pictures of Wittgenstein's thought. To the extent that anyone reads the work of the later Wittgenstein as a dogmatic or theoretical treatise instead of as a methodological turn, he cannot fail to find Ludwig Wittgenstein hopelessly confused and obscure. But if Wittgenstein is read with a methodological eye, if his work is seen as a series of hints and pushes geared to change our whole perspective, then his truly radical design for philosophical activity is clear and striking. This methodological hermeneutic conceives his work as a pattern of exercises designed to dissolve certain puzzles and to bring about the continuing linguistic self-awareness which must become the "foundation" for all inquiry.

In a sense the Wittgenstein shift can be understood as analogous to Immanuel Kant's transcendental revolution.[9] Kant's revolutionary foundations were the result of a turn to the psychological subject. Thought reflecting on itself could discover its own boundaries and grounds. Kant claimed to have thus discovered the universal categories which structure our minds and dictate how we perceive the world. He concludes that problems in philosophy arise when thought goes beyond its limits by attempting to know what it cannot by its very constitution know. Knowing how we know reveals that the extension of scientific thinking into metaphysical realms is a confusion of the limits of each area. Metaphysics, then, must give up any scientific pretensions. Wittgenstein too wants to draw limits because he too believes that philosophy gets into trouble when it strays beyond its proper bounds and into the scientific. But Wittgenstein calls for a critique of the linguistic subject. Kant carried the anthropocentric revolution forward but stopped with the categories of the mind. Wittgenstein claims that one must go further: it is the particular "categories" of our language which structure all inquiry. There is a realization that it is not some internal reality (such as mental categories) or some external reality (such as the supposed immediacy of an already-out-there-now-real) which is fundamentally determinative, but rather language. Attention to language surfaces the boudaries and limits of philosophical discussion. Going beyond these limits can be confusing. Thus both Kant and Wittgenstein opened a new era in philosophy; both sought to end confusion by setting limits to philosophy; both looked to the subject for their grounding. Yet their procedure and conclusions are decidedly different. For Ludwig Wittgenstein, the starting point and the ground of inquiry is to be found not in thought but in language and not in a new psychological or linguistic foundation but in radical rejection of the search for foundations.

Wittgenstein's intent was very much to set philosophy in a new direction; his work turns around the question of foundations. But using the term "foundational" in regard to Wittgenstein's thought is markedly dangerous. His work is foundational in that it is concerned with the basics of fruitful philosophical inquiry. It is linguistic in that it consistently looks to language for these basics. Wittgenstein, both early and late, wanted to move philosophical inquiry away from the established traditions of epistemology and metaphysics and toward an elucidation of language. But this concern with foundations and language is transformed in his later period. Wittgenstein became thoroughly anti-foundational; he rejected the search for foundations even as he himself had once conceived it in the Tractatus. He rejected as self-deception the philosophical search for privileged representations or mental processes to guarantee our knowledge. The project of the early Wittgenstein was the construction of a new linguistic foundation for knowledge; the project of the later Wittgenstein was warning others about the wrong-headedness of such a project. Not only is it fruitless, but looking for such a foundational experience, representation, or process causes us to overlook the jobs really done by language. In short, Ludwig Wittgenstein's discussion of foundations ends in a rejection of the entire quest. It is accurate, then, to describe Wittgenstein as interested in the foundations of inquiry, only if one recalls that the term "foundational" also describes the very positions and approaches which he finds radically self-defeating.[10]

The new Copernican revolution in philosophy, the final critique, is constituted by attention to the words and sentences of our ordinary language. For Ludwig Wittgenstein, the source of philosophical problems is the bewitchment of our minds by language. His work is an organized resistance to this bewitchment. The later Wittgenstein wants to attack the various diseases which grip us and to cure us by means of a motley linguistic therapy which constantly and continuously brings us back to our everyday usage. His method is to work through sample philosophical muddles and to dissolve them by attending to their context in ordinary language. Plodding through his workbooks is intended to bring us to a new awareness of our own language and thereby to relax our present philosophical consternation and make us more immune to the confusion inherent in doing philosophy. The later Wittgenstein sets out examples of confusion and leads us through them until we have learned how to guide ourselves.

> In teaching you philosophy I'm like a guide showing you how to find your way round London. I have to take you through the city from north to south, from east to west, from Euston to the embankment and from Piccadilly to the Marble Arch. After I have taken you many journeys through the city, in all sorts of directions, we shall have passed through any given street a number of times. . . . At the end of this tour you will know London; you will be able to find your way about like a born Londoner.[11]

There is no theory here, but only the development of a habit of linguistic attentiveness by repeated and directed exposure to philosophical knots. The point of this therapy is to get to know one's way about in the world by getting to know one's way about language: the Delphian "Know Thyself" has been further specified to "Know Thy Language-game." The result is dissolution of real philosophical knots. In this way Wittgenstein would cure a sickness of mind which bedevils philosophy.

Such a cure could also be of use to philosophically inclined theology. But it is not a theology or religion. As we shall see, Wittgenstein's approach cannot be construed to imply a theology that is merely the analysis of language. Neither does it provide convenient philosophical justification for one's religious fideism. It does not imply any particular substantive theological positions. It does provide various therapies. Wittgenstein sought non-theoretical dissolutions of some of the knots with which professional thinkers have bound us. His work is an escape from foundations, an escape from confusing grammatical analogies and imposed pictures of our language. By curing our tendency to confuse, Witgenstein can help us clear up muddles without simply offering another system as that cure. This is what the theologian needs from Wittgenstein: perspective, not dogma.

This then is the Wittgenstein with whom we would have a revisionist theology dialogue. It is not the Wittgenstein of the earlier <u>Tractatus</u> period, who was fascinated with the possibilities for a scientific philosophy allowed by logical atomism. It is not the Wittgenstein of his more phenomenological period, who sought empirical verification of the elementary units of language in the direct awareness of phenomenological data. It is the mature Wittgenstein of the <u>Investigations</u> period, who worked a devastating critique of both of these earlier phases and turned method in philosophy into empirical linguistic self-awareness.[12] In attempting to formulate a Wittgenstein theology, our procedure will be to begin with an understanding of Ludwig Wittgenstein derived directly from Wittgenstein's own work, and not from just any pieces of that work, but from what he considered to be its culmination--the <u>Philosophische Untersuchungen</u>. The <u>Philosophical Investigations</u> is the touchstone of the Wittgenstein corpus. His writings before Philosophical Investigations can be viewed as stages on the way to it and those after the Investigations as further applications of the method presented most fully there.[13] The linguistic philosophy it preaches by its practice is the core of Wittgenstein's legacy.[14]

In the Philosophical Investigations we see that Wittgenstein's philosophy is not a system to be adopted or memorized. It is an activity and a perspective to be learned from a workbook and verified in the actual clarification of important problems. By means of this workbook its reader is to be converted to a consistent sort of linguistic awareness. Wittgenstein sought to bring about conversion to a new perspective on philosophical problems and therein to ground philosophical inquiry. This conversion is a turn in a radically new direction. It is not a convoluted theory but merely the habit of looking in a simple and obvious place for solutions.

> It is as if a man is standing in a room facing a wall on which are painted a number of dummy doors. Wanting to get out, he fumblingly tries to open them, vainly trying them all, one after the other, over and over again. But of course, it is quite useless. And all the time, although he doesn't realize it, there is a real door in the wall behind his back, and all he has to do is turn around and open it. To help him get out of the room all we have to do is get him to look in a different direction. But it's hard to do this, since, wanting to get out, he resists our attempts to turn him away from where he thinks the exit must be.[15]

We must quit tugging on the same old doors and turn about in order to see the real way out of our philosophical confinement. But conversion to a new picture is not a function of any theoretical argument. After all, theoretical arguments have meaning and validity only within their given picture or framework. In seeking to change precisely this framework, one can hardly expect that arguments which are not grounded in the old governing picture will be accepted or understood by those within that picture. Yet to ground one's argument in that very picture under attack would be self-defeating and contradictory. So it is not a question of a battle between two theories anchored in the same paradigm, but rather a matter of attempting to shift that very basis for validity. This is done by showing the new perspective at work and in the process leading the reader to discover its value and fruitfulness for herself. This view of method as an activity and a mind-set denies the fundamental relevance of propounding conclusions and theses. But if the best way to grasp Wittgenstein's method is to see it at work, is there any place for a general exposition of his thought?

It is true that expositions of Wittgenstein's thought are troublesome. Since they are a medium not fully appropriate to his message, they risk accidentally confirming the misapprehension that he is simply another theorist, further obscuring the non-theoretical, non-dogmatic nature of his method. For Wittgenstein the validity of his linguistic perspective cannot be established by discussing its history and development. He provides a new way of viewing things, a new perspective or horizon which as such cannot be learned in a theoretical statement but only emerges in the sensitive examination of concrete cases. Only in the practical wrestling with particular knots can his linguistic philosophy display its appropriateness and effectiveness. The concrete case of David Tracy's revisionist theology will provide such a particular fuel. At the same time, it will provide an opportunity for Wittgenstein to move into a sophisticated theological context. This is the properly Wittgenstein procedure. However, given the various interpretations of the direction and achievement of Ludwig Wittgenstein's later work, a broad survey of his thought is a necessary--though perhaps non-Wittgensteinian--preparation which will also serve to fix the parameters of our theological investigation. Although Wittgenstein's method is an instance in which "the proof is in the pudding," a general orientation to Wittgensteinian cookery may prove a useful preliminary.

The first step in an explanation of later Wittgenstein is an explanation of early Wittgenstein. Wittgenstein's thought is an organic and developing whole. One has not grasped it if she never goes beyond the period of the Tractatus Logico-Philosophicus or the Philosophical Remarks. At the same time, one cannot really claim to understand the Philosophical Investigations without marking its relation to Wittgenstein's earlier positions. Our concern here is with the later Wittgenstein. But Wittgenstein himself begins his Investigations by remarking that only in the light of the Tractarian view of language and philosophy does that of the Investigations emerge clearly.

> Four years ago I had occasion to re-read my first book (the Tractatus Logico-Philosophicus) and to explain its ideas to someone. It suddenly seemed to me that I should publish those thoughts and the new ones together: that the latter could be seen in the right light only by contrast with and against the background of my old way of thinking.[16]

The two foci of Wittgenstein's thought are represented by the Tractatus and the Investigations.[17] The key to understanding Wittgenstein is to understand the continuity and the discontinuity of these two periods. It is true that the first rule for the interpretation of the later Wittgenstein's philosophy is to recognize its therapeutic style and intent. But the second requirement is to recognize that the target of this therapy is the early Wittgenstein himself. Thus any portrait of the later Wittgenstein must have the Tractatus as its background. The Philosophical Investigations is an attack upon the theoretical, a priori philosophizing and the most rigorous example of such a philosophy is Wittgenstein's own Tractatus Logico-Philosophicus.

67

The Background: Meaning and Method in the Early Years

The Logisch-Philosophische Abhandlung is a laconic piece of just eighty pages. Though it can be read in an hour or so, it cannot so easily be understood, for one finds there a novel treatment of various troublesome philosophical themes including logic, ontology, and ethics. It would be folly to pretend to deal adequately with such complex issues in just the next few pages. Fortunately our interest is limited to a focus on method and in particular to the value of the Tractatus in understanding the methodological concerns of the Philosophical Investigations. This will govern the shape of our exposition. However, such a focus should not be seen as arbitrary. The various substantive philosophical issues taken up in the Tractatus are subordinate to its governing methodological thrust. That is to say, the business of Tractatus is the construction and validation of a very specific metaphilosophical position. The Tractatus Logico-Philosophicus is concerned with the foundations of philosophy.

Of course it is natural that the shape of Wittgenstein's methodological pursuits be dictated by his intellectual milieu. That milieu included two strands which might be loosely called the logical and the ethical. While studying engineering he had developed an interest in the foundations of mathematics. His exploration of these questions brought him to Bertrand Russell's Principles of Mathematics and exposed him as well to the similar work of Gottlob Frege. Once at Cambridge other influences included mathematician Frank Ramsey and G. E. Moore. Logical and mathematical questions were a major stimulus for the early Wittgenstein.[18] It is within this context that Wittgenstein worked out his solution to what has been shown[19] to have been the typical ethical concerns of is fin-de-siècle Vienna. This background provides the other rein on Wittgenstein's thought. It explains the central Tractarian concern to preserve the important realms of religion, ethics and the like from the omnivorous jaws of scientism. His is a classical, almost Kantian attempt to separate and secure fact and value by setting the limits of each. The Tractatus revolves around this fixing of boundaries as to what can and cannot be said.[20] However, while such an ethical vision may have provided the impetus for a project like the Tractatus, it was the logical and theoretical context of Cambridge philosophy which governed its actual form. The program of the Tractatus is unavailable and unintelligible apart from these peculiar discussions of logic and mathematics.

For Wittgenstein the proper approach to philosophical problems is through logic and language. Here is the critical core of philosophy.

> The book deals with the problems of philosophy, and shows, I believe, that the reason why these problems are posed is that the basic logic of our

language is misunderstood.[21]

One brings clarity to philosophical thinking by surveying and marking out its proper territory. Since thought is not directly and fully accesible, this is done by drawing limits to its expression in language. "In a proposition a thought finds an expression that can be perceived by the senses."[22] Wittgenstein drives this examination back to the basic question of logic: How is it that propositions can tell us about the world?[23] Given the certainty possible in logic and mathematics, what sort of underlying structure can one infer? Logic is the point of departure for an investigation which reveals the limits operative in the linguistic expression of thought and thereby refocuses the philosopher's problematic. The Tractatus proceeds by first uncovering the limits-of language and then noting the limits-to language. The limits-of language are discovered by inferring the structure of the relationship between the world and the proposition. This view of the essential nature and structure of language will then allow one to draw the limits-to language, i.e., to note what can and what cannot be said. Thus the philosopher's house is set in order.

The Tractatus proposes an a priori approach to philosophical foundations. It appeals not to experience but to logic. It seeks that order which is present before all experience. It proceeds by inferring what must be the grounding structure and possibilities of our language. As Wittgenstein remarked in his Notebooks:

> The great problem round which everything that I write turns is: Is there an order in the world a priori, and if so what does it consist in?[24]

The Tractatus is an attempt to discover such an order. The limits-of and the limits-to our language constitute an a priori skeleton which provides the possibility of clarity, accuracy and certainty. We and others do know exactly what we mean, and what we mean can be absolutely true or false. Why is this so? There is an a priori order to the world and it is reflected in language. Wittgenstein begins with the problem of explaining the nature of the proposition. The working out of this relationship between the proposition and the world yields the Tractatus theory of meaning and its concomitant version of the philosophical enterprise.

Wittgenstein's central problem, then, was how language and thought could be related to reality.[25] The key philosophical question became "what does the logical identity of sign and thing signified really consist in?"[26] The solution to this problem was Wittgenstein's intuition that thought and language must picture reality.[27]

> The general concept of the proposition carries with it a quite general concept of the coordination of proposition and situation: the solution to all my questions must be extremely simple.
> In the proposition a world is as it were put together

> experimentally. (As when in the law-court in Paris a motor-car accident is represented by means of dolls, etc.)[28]
>
> A proposition is a picture of reality.
> A proposition is a model of reality as we imagine it.[29]

A sentence is a picture because it represents reality in exactly the same manner as a photograph or map: there is a one to one correspondence between the elements of the picture and the facts of the situation. Furthermore, the things the picture stands for are related in the same way as the picture shows them. This picturing function is to be taken quite literally. The sentence "my fork is to the left of my knife" literally depicts the state of affairs in a table setting. That is, in the proposition itself the word "fork" appears to the left of the word "knife." This is, of course, an unusally direct depiction in which one spatial relation represents another. There are many other (non-spatial) modes in which such a situation might be transcribed.[30] But this example does indicate the sort of literal correlation proposed by the picture theory. A sentence is a model of reality. All language functions by mirroring objects in relation in the world.

Not all sentences are straightforward; our language often disguises its pictorial logic. This is not surprising as everyday language is a complex product of a complicated human organism. Its purpose is not to make its pictorial nature obvious but simply to function in communication.[31] Yet, however veiled, the essential convention of language is picturing.

> At first sight a proposition--one set out on the printed page, for example--does not seem to be a picture of the reality with which it is concerned. But neither do written notes seem at first sight to be a picture of a piece of music, nor our phonetic notation (the alphabet) to be a picture of our speech.
> And yet these sign-languages prove to be pictures, even in the ordinary sense, of what they represent.[32]

Naturally complex propositions and language do reveal their simple pictorial structure under philosophical analysis.

Fundamentally the picture theory demands that both language and the world must have definite structures. These structures must be identical and must somehow be hooked up to each other. Such structures are discovered not by attending to the world but by analyzing propositions.

Analysis discovers how it is that such picturing can take place.

Inference tells us that the complex propositions which occur in speech can be broken down into the more elementary propositions which they presume. The various propositions of our language stand upon a matrix of other simpler propositions. The fact of communication suggests that there must be some end to this analysis, some final propositions which cannot be further analyzed. These are elementary propositions, propositions which picture the world and which allow other propositions to do the same. Elementary propositions consist not of other propositions but of names in concatenation.[33] These names are simple and yield to no analysis: "A name cannot be dissected any further by means of definitions: it is a primitive sign."[34] Here is the point at which language is in direct contact with reality. "A name means an object. The object is its meaning."[35] Names go proxy for simple objects in the world.

> One name stands for one thing, another for another thing, and they are combined with one another. In this way the whole group--like a tableau vivant--presents a state of affairs.[36]

Names in concatenation parallel objects in relation. Names do not picture but are the basic cells from which the pictures of elementary propositions are built. The combination of simple names constitutes an elementary proposition, elementary propositions ground complex propositions, and the totality of propositions is language. The world <u>must</u> have a concomitant structure.

The objects to which simple names refer must also be absolutely simple. "Objects make up the substances of the world. That is why they cannot be composite."[37] They are the ultimate particles of the world and as such must subsist independent of what is actually the case at any given time.[38] "Objects are what is unalterable and subsistent; their configuration is what is changing and unstable."[39] All of this is non-empirical deduction. These simples are needed as partners to the ultimate constituents of language. Wittgenstein was well aware of the difficulty of providing any samples of a simple object, but insisted that their existence was, nevertheless, logically necessary for the working of language.

> It seems that the idea of the <u>simple</u> is already to be found contained in that of the complex and in the idea of analysis, and in such a way that we come to this idea quite apart from any examples of simple objects, or of propositions which mention them, and we realize the existence of the simple object--a priori--as a logical necessity.[40]

When these simples are combined, contingent states of affairs arise. This arrangement of simple objects is what is represented by elementary propositions. A state of affairs is a group of objects in a determinate relationship. The totality of such determinate relationships is the world.

But though both the world and language may have definite structures, how are these two structures related? The elements of a picture must be related to one another in a determinate way in order for it to be a picture.[41] The elements of reality must be related to one another in a determinate way in order for there to be a world. The picture and the world each have a logical form, a particular structure. They describe a particular possible combination within the parameters of logical space. In order for a picture to picture reality the same logical form must be held in common.[42] When the determinate relationship of the picture's elements is the same as the determinate relationship of the world's elements, then the former and the latter can be said to have a pictorial relationship.

> What any picture, of whatever form, must have in common with reality, in order to be able to depict it--correctly or incorrectly--in any way at all, is logical form, i.e., the form of reality.[43]

This means that not only do pictures represent the elements (objects) of the world, but that these elements are represented in relationship. Names represent objects directly and logical form allows elementary propositions to show these objects in relationship.

> In a picture the elements of the picture are the representatives of objects.[44]

> The fact that the elements of a picture are related to one another in a determinate way represents that things are related to one another in the same way.[45]

Thus a picture represents a possible state of affairs in the world. This is to say that it has sense. It is a further question to ask if this picture is true as well. Are the objects really related in this way? This question of truth is not a function of the internal logic of picturing but of comparison with reality.[46] A meaningful sentence simply presents a possible state of affairs in the world; it pictures in a rather definite way. Its ability to picture depends upon the parallel structure of language and the world and the necessity of sharing logical form.

There remains the issue of how these structures are actually joined. There is no point in talking about the truth or falsity of a proposition unless propositions have the possibility of being extremely accurate in their account of the world. In order for a proposition to really be a picture of reality its correlation with the world must be precise. The exact state of affairs posited must be expressed in an equally definite picture. We have already seen that this is possible because the definite structure of the picture is capable of reflecting the definite structure of the world. But how are these two definite structures to be accurately related? What sort of correlation would allow the necessary precision?

Wittgenstein is sure that there must be a correlation of the picture's elements with things. That is, names and objects must somehow be in direct contact. Names must be able to relate to their objects with pinpoint accuracy. This is how sentences mean.

> These correlations are, as it were, the feelers of the picture's elements, with which the picture touches reality.[47]

> That is how a picture is attached to reality, it reaches right out to do it.[48]

An elementary proposition is a projection of a possible state of affairs in the world. There are "lines of projection" between the basics of language and the basics of the world. Furthermore, whatever this projection is which proposes to link facts and propositions, it seems to be given in thinking:

> We use the perceptible sign of a proposition (spoken, written, etc.) as a projection of a possible situation.

> The method of projection is to think of the sense of the proposition.[49]

Thought must add enormously much that is not said to each proposition.[50] What it does add hooks up names and objects in a manner that excludes any fuzziness of meaning. "The watch is lying on the table" is vague; "lying on the table" bears many interpretations and describes several states of affairs. But in actual use the meaning of this sentence is certain and limited. There is a sharpness of meaning, a definiteness of correlation that is supplied by our meaning it, by our intention. "It seems clear that what we MEAN must always be 'sharp.'"[51] Our ordinary language may be vague but our world is not; what we mean is a quite precise and specific arrangement of elements. Two definite structures are linked by a mental process which correlates names in concatenation with objects in combination and does so in such a precise manner that each can reflect the same logical form. The lines of correlation necessary for picturing are drawn in thought. Intention compensates for any lack of linguistic definiteness. Wittgenstein is sure that these lines of projection, however tangled and hidden, must stretch from the elements of language to the elements of the world. This is why language works. Thus the proposition and thought cooperate to fashion a picture of reality.[52]

There is, then, a structure in the world a priori. This structure is derived from the a priori structure of language as revealed in analysis. Language is made up of complex propositions which are composed of elementary propositions which in turn are the result of a combination of names. These names are in direct contact with the subsistent objects of reality. That reality has an identical structure. The gross facts which make up the world are composed of atomic facts which in turn are the result of the combination of simple objects. These objects are in direct contact with the names which constitute elementary propositions. The sharing of a logical-pictorial form allows certain lines of correlation to tie the most fundamental elements of our language to those of our world. All other propositions are truth-functions of elementary propositions. All that is the case in the world is a function of the atomic facts. Whether or not a state of affairs posited by a particular elementary proposition is true is a matter of fact, i.e., of comparison with the world.[53] In this way propositions tell us about the world. The essence of language, the essence of the world, and their essential correlation are woven into a new foundation for the business of philosophy. The boundaries and task of philosophy are redescribed by this a priori theory of meaning.

The focal point of the <u>Tractatus</u> is not at all the picture theory. The point of the <u>Tractatus</u> is to end the confusing over-extension of philosophy's competence. This can only be done once it is disclosed that meaning and truth are, in differing ways, a function of the correspondence of word and world. If the limits of language are as the picture theory would suppose, then one has a measure for drawing limits to language. Transgressing these limits is the real genesis of many traditional philosophical problems. Wittgenstein finds it philosophically important to explain how what can be said is said.

> Now I'm afraid you haven't really got hold of my main contention, to which the whole business of logical propositions is only a corollary. The main point is the theory of what can be expressed (<u>gesagt</u>) by propositions—i.e., by language—(and, which comes to the same, what can be <u>thought</u>) and what can not be expressed by propositions, but only shown; which, I belive, is the cardinal problem of philosophy.[54]

What can be expressed by a proposition must be marked off from what cannot be so expressed but only shown. Because of the way propositions mean they are fundamentally descriptive. Indeed, the best example of what can be said is natural science.[55] A proposition which purports to talk of matters that cannot be described in the world, to carry a burden beyond that which propositional structures can bear, is merely a pseudo-proposition. It appears to be functioning as a proposition (picturing) but in reality it does not mean; it is not supposed to be a picture of anything in the world. Such pseudo-propositions are found to constitute many of the traditional concerns of philosophy.

The world is a contingent state of affairs accessible in accord with the limits of language. A proposition has sense if it proposes a situation in the world. To say that something cannot be said is to say that it is not in the realm of the factual. Logic, mathematics, and the a priori laws of science are not about the world at all. They are a priori, tautologous, and say nothing. They show the form and relationships that must obtain among elements, but do not themselves have any one to one correspondence with any element of the world.[56] Their formal message is shown in the structure of what can be said, but cannot itself be said. "What can be shown, cannot be said."[57]

The propositions of metaphysics, religion, ethics, and aesthetics also fall under the category of what can be shown but not said. They concern not just what is at the edges of the world and language but what is completely beyond them.[58]

> The sense of the world must lie outside the world. In the world everything is as it is, and everything happens as it does happen: <u>in</u> it no value exists--and if it did exist, it would have no value.
> If there is any value that does have value, it must lie outside the whole sphere of what happens and is the case. For all that happens and is the case is accidental.
> What makes it non-accidental cannot lie <u>within</u> the world, since if it did it would itself be accidental.[59]

Propositions indicate only how things happen to be in the world but not why they must be that way. The sense and purpose of the world is beyond the world. It cannot be said. Attempts to express it in language result in pseudo-propositions and are examples of nonsense. Yet this latter nonsense--what Wittgenstein calls the mystical--is exactly what is most important in life. It is this unwritten side of the <u>Tractatus</u> which Wittgenstein thinks to be the most significant.[60]

What can be said (natural science) can be said clearly. What cannot be said (the mystical) can be shown. Attempts to say what can only be shown confuse these two distinct functions of language, jam and distort the calculus of meaning, and therefore issue in nonsense. The whole of the <u>Tractatus Logico-Philosophicus</u> is clearly and dramatically summarized by its final proposition: "What we cannot speak about we must pass over in silence."[61] This is the primary lesson of the <u>Tractatus</u>. A corollary lesson is the nature of philosophical inquiry.

What is left for philosophy to do after the <u>Tractatus</u>? What sort of philosophy is the <u>Tractatus</u> itself? Philosophy gives us no picture of reality. Philosophy cannot confirm or confute any scientific investigation.[62] It is not one of the natural sciences; it does not deal with what can be said nor should it try to say what cannot be said. Philosophy is an activity, a display, a showing. It shows the source of its problems: it can display the essential nature of language and expose pseudo-propositions.

> The correct method in philosophy would really be the following: to say nothing except what can be said, i.e., propositions of natural science--i.e., something that has nothing to do with philosophy--and then, whenever someone else wanted to say something metaphysical, to demonstrate to him that he had failed to give a meaning to certain signs in his propositions. Although it would not be satisfying to the other person--he would not have the feeling that we were teaching him philosophy--this method would be the only correct one.[63]

Philosophy is no longer a body of doctrine or a system but rather it is an activity. It is not a collection of propositions or thoughts but the clarifying of propositions and thoughts. Philosophy is not an organic whole but a series of ad hoc attacks anchored in the picture theory of meaning. The goal of this activity is to help troubled philosophers see and respect the boundaries of language which they continually violate. Analysis of philosophical propositions often discovers that they contain a sign to which no meaning has been given. Philosophy exposes such veiled nonsense and the pseudo-problems it generates. Thus philosophy is simply the elucidation of meaning. The doing of philosophy becomes the activity of clarifying thought and language by giving them sharp boundaries.[64]

The propositions of the Tractatus are not exempt from this philosophical analysis. The Tractatus presents clearly what can be said in order to show what is inexpressible. But this presentation consists in propositions about logic, language, thought, which are exactly the sort which it claims cannot be meaningfully expressed. If we grasp what the Tractatus claims to say, then we see why on its own grounds this cannot really be said. If the argument of the Tractatus is correct, then the Tractatus itself is disclosed as nonsensical. Wittgenstein's propositions are about the edges of the world and language. They cannot have meaning as defined by the very theory which they put forth. By their own definition they cannot say anything. They can of course show us a great deal and this is precisely Wittgenstein's point. Analysis of the philosophical propositions of the Tractatus reveals that they say nothing but that they do display the boundaries and procedures of philosophical discourse. In short, the propositions of the Tractatus are a negative: they demonstrate what they falsely attempt to say. Their positive content consists in what they cannot say. The process of analysis which constitutes the Tractatus transports the attentive reader to a summit from which the a priori structure of the world and language is visible and from which, consequently, she can order the philosophical chaos below.

> My propositions serve as elucidations in the following way: anyone who understands me eventually recognizes them as nonsensical when he

> has used them--as steps--to climb up beyond them.
> (He must, so to speak, throw away the ladder after
> he has climbed up it.)
> He must transcend these propositions, and then
> he will see the world aright.[65]

The Tractatus is self-destructive, but it is a very instructive suicide. The failure of its propositions is their success. It is only when we understand why Wittgenstein should not have said what he tries to say that we understand what he wants to show us.

Thus we have seen both the driving issues of Wittgenstein's thought and the particular shape of their first resolution. (1) The Logisch-Philosophische Abhandlung is a methodological treatise. It wants to demonstrate that philosophy is a method, not a doctrine.[66] It reveals philosophy as the ad hoc elucidation of philosophical propositions by means of specially grounded analysis. It is an activity. (2) This analysis is justified by a certain picture of the connection of thought, language, and the world. (3) Thus philosophy is to be focused on the problem of meaning. Philosophy is to be a method of linguistic attentiveness. (4) One can appropriate this new awareness by working through a guidebook such as Wittgenstein provides. (5) These general issues of the Tractatus find their specific implementation in the development of the picture theory of meaning and its logical atomism. (6) The necessity requisite for such a scientific philosophy seems to demand that language operate as an exact calculus in a manner determined a priori. The precision of the relationship between the world and language and thought is Wittgenstein's key problem. The picture theory of meaning is his solution in the Tractatus. This theory is essentialist, a priori, and mechanical. It presumes that language, thought, and the world must be related in a one-to-one correlation. (7) Language can mirror the world because its determinate structure and that of the world are mirror images finely attuned by the mental process of intending. (8) This picture theory of meaning supports a philosophy that is a recalling of the foundational limits of language in order to avoid transgressing the limits to what can be said. Attending to the a priori structure and boundaries of meaning is the antidote for the feverish confusion characteristic of philosophical speculation. The Tractatus begins with the assumption that setting the limits-to language is a matter of discovering its essential nature. This investigation is developed into the picture theory of meaning which in turn becomes the basis for philosophical elucidations.

The issue of meaning and philosophical method remained central for the mature Wittgenstein as well. However, the Tractarian realization of this project was razed and the ruins became the foundation for a new philosophy that was not at all a priori but rather rigorously a posteriori. The search for foundations had self-destructed.

Notes

1. Wittgenstein's "Lectures on Religious Belief" are merely notes from students. There are some longer remarks in the Nachlass, but these too are unfinished and not intended for publication. His review of Frazer's Golden Bough is not really developed, but there are clues to be found there. Wittgenstein does occasionally mention religion or theology in other works, but much too much is made of these scant references; they are certainly not composed for theologians. Furthermore, for reasons internal to Wittgenstein's project, we are not really concerned with Wittgenstein's own conclusions on religion, but rather with the import of his philosophical method for certain philosophical issues in fundamental theology. The focus is to be on how to clear up muddles.

2. Richard B. Braithwaite, An Empiricist's View of the Nature of Religious Beliefs (Cambridge: Cambridge University Press, 1955); Paul M. van Buren, The Secular Meaning of the Gospel (New York: Macmillan Press, 1963).

3. Dewi Zaphaniah Phillips, Faith and Philosophical Enquiry (London: Routledge & Kegan Paul, 1970); Peter Winch, "Understanding a Primitive Society" in Bryan Wilson, ed., Rationality (New York: Harper & Row, 1970), pp. 78-111. The tag "fideist" is suggested by Kai Neilsen, "Wittgensteinian Fideism," Philosophy 42 (July 1967): 191-209. The fideist or relativist interpretation of Wittgenstein has come to the fore more recently in the interesting argument of Roger Trigg, Reason and Commitment (Cambridge: Cambridge University Press, 1973).

4. Jerry H. Gill, "Saying and Showing: Radical Themes in Wittgenstein's On Certainty," Religious Studies 10 (September 1974): 279-90. See also the review of Trigg, Reason by John H. Whittaker, "Wittgenstein and Religion: Some Later Views of His Later Works," Religious Studies Review 4 (July 1978): 188-93. It is now generally recognized that Wittgenstein was not a positivist, though even the members of the Vienna Circle considered him so for a time. "A whole generation of disciples was able to take Wittgenstein for a positivist because he has something of enormous importance in common with the positivist: he draws the line between what we can speak about and what we must be silent about just as they do. The difference is only that they have nothing to be silent about. Positivism holds--and this is its essence--that what we can speak about is all that matters in life. Whereas Wittgenstein passionately believes that all that really matters in human life is precisely what, in his view, we must be silent about." Paul Englemann. Letters From Ludwig Wittgenstein, With a Memoir, trans. L. Furtmuller, ed. B. McGuiness (Oxford: Basail Blackwell, 1967), p. 97.

5. This is typical of David Burrell's use of Wittgenstein as for example in his "Theology and the Linguistic Turn," Communio 6 (Spring 1979): 95-112.

6. Anders Nygren, Meaning and Method: Prolegomena to a Scientific Philosophy of Religion and a Scientific Theology, trans. Philip S. Watson (Philadelphia: Fortress Press, 1972).

7. Norman Malcom, Ludwig Wittgenstein: A Memoir (London: Oxford University Press, 1972), p. 63. G. H. von Wright confirms this in his "Biographical Sketch" included in Malcom, Memoir, p. 1: "He was of the opinion--justified, I believe—that his ideas were usually misunderstood and distorted even by those who professed to be his disciples." Those interested in a brief introduction to the life and thought of Ludwig Wittgenstein should consult Norman Malcolm, "Wittgenstein," in Paul Edwards, ed., The Encyclopedia of Philosophy.

8. The proliferation of literature on the meaning of "form of life" and whether religion is a form of life is amazing and largely misdirected. This obsession is an attempt to appropriate Wittgenstein. But the proper role for the concept "form of life" is merely that of a tool that comes to one when he needs it and not that of an enduring theory. The discussion is put in its place by John Whittaker in his excellent piece, "Language-Games and Forms of Life Unconfused," Philosophical Investigations 1 (Fall 1978): 39-48. The problem with drawing out the metaphysics or philosophy of language implied in Wittgenstein's work is not that it cannot be done, but that it distracts one from Wittgenstein's real point and confuses his interpretation.

9. David Pears, Ludwig Wittgenstein (New York: Penguin Books, 1977), pp. 2-35 and passim; Erik Stenius, Wittgenstein's "Tractatus:" A Critical Exposition of Its Main Line of Thought (Oxford: Basil Blackwell, 1960), pp. 214-26.

10. For an excellent account of the historic damage done by the search for philosophical foundations and the possible antidote by Wittgenstein, see Richard Rorty, Philosophy and the Mirror of Nature (Princton: Princeton University Press, 1979). I continue to use the word "foundational" exactly because it is double-edged. It recalls Wittgenstein's philosophical attack point and yet it also indicates the point at which Wittgenstein's philosophy can be inserted into the established categories for doing theology.

11. Reported in D. A. T. Gasking and A. C. Jackson, "Wittgenstein as a Teacher," in K. T. Fann, ed., Ludwig Wittgenstein: The Man and His Philosophy (New York: Dell Publishing Co., 1967; reprint ed., Atlantic Highlands, New Jersey: Humanities Press, 1978), p. 51.

12. A study of the historical development and context of Wittgenstein's thought is beyond the scope of our strictly philosophical and theological study. The historical literature cannot validate Wittgenstein's point of view, but it can help one to understand that view. One might begin with the following: Garth L. Hallet, A Companion to Wittgenstein's "Philosophical Investigations," (Ithaca: Cornell University

Press, 1977), pp. 23-57; Hallett, *Wittgenstein's Definition of Meaning as Use* (New York: Fordham University Press, 1967); Anthony Kenny, *Wittgenstein* (Cambridge: Harvard University Press, 1974); Allan Janik and Stephen Toulmin, *Wittgenstein's Vienna* (New York: Simon and Schuster, 1973). For an introduction to Wittgenstein's phenomenological period see Rush Rhees, *Discussions of Wittgenstein* (London: Routledge & Kegan Paul, 1970), pp. 16-22; Herbert Spiegelberg, "The Puzzle of Ludwig Wittgenstein's Phanomenologie (1929-?)," *American Philosophical Quarterly* 5 (October 1968): 224-56. Also of interest is Robert L. Arrington, "Wittgenstein and Phenomenology," *Philosophy Today* 22 (Summer 1978): 287-300. A recent study of Wittgenstein and the phenomenological tradition is Nicholas F. Gier, *Wittgenstein and Phenomenology: A Comparative Study of the Later Wittgenstein, Husserl, Heidegger, and Merleau-Ponty* (Albany: State University of New York Press, 1981). The best introduction to the issues is to be found in Garth Hallett's unpublished lecture, "Wittgenstein and the Failure of Phenomenology," Loyola University, Chicago (Fall, 1969).

13. For example, the *Tractatus* of the early period was improved upon in *Philosophical Remarks* and *Philosophical Grammar* and in the manuscripts of the middle period. The failure of these efforts eventually developed into the mature position represented by *Philosophical Invetigations*. Wittgenstein's work after his *summa* can be seen as an application of its basic perspective to other issues and areas as, for example, in the papers recently published as *On Certainty* and *On Colour*.

14. It is to be noted that we will not be concerned with an historical proof for our interpretation of Wittgenstein. For reasons that will become clear, the value or disvalue of the view we are labeling Wittgensteinian must be shown by observing it actually at work. It is not established or validated by historical argument, though it may be best understood against its historical context. Our interest is only in as much background as is needed to understand what we call Wittgenstein's method. But the value of this method for doing theology will not lie in its origin in Ludwig Wittgenstein, but in its actual usefulness. Hence a full historical discussion of the development of Wittgenstein's thought is not to the point.

15. Gasking and Jackson, "Wittgenstein as a Teacher," p. 52.

16. *PI*, p. vi. "A considerable part of the *Investigations* is an attack, either explicit or implicit, on the earlier work. This development is probably unique in the history of philosophy—a thinker producing, at different periods of his life, two highly original systems of thought, each system the result of many years of intensive labors, each expressed in an elegant and powerful style, each greatly influencing contemporary philosophy, and the second being a criticism and rejection of the first." Malcolm, "Wittgenstein," p. 334.

17. These are the only two major works which he wanted published.

Furthermore, the Tractatus and the Investigations can be understood as symbols for and summaries of two distinct views of philosophy. The tendencies they represent are not to be considered limited to their pages. It was a Tractatus-like approach that was Wittgenstein's target, not just his own formulation of it. Our discussion of Wittgenstein depends heavily on the Tractatus and its preliminary Notebooks and on the Investigations and its preliminary studies The Blue and Brown Books. In discussing these works our focus will not be the exposition of the particular problems they treat but the new perspective behind the dissolution of these problems.

18. "I will only mention that I am indebted to Frege's great works and to the writing of my friend Mr. Bertrand Russell for much of the stimulation of my thoughts." T, p. 3. For more on this context see Pears, Wittgenstein, pp. 39-50; Kenny, Wittgenstein, pp. 19-53; G. E. M. Anscombe, An Introduction to Wittgenstein's "Tractatus" (London: Hutchinson University Library, 1959), pp. 12-20, 98-112.

19. See Janik and Toulmin, Vienna. They demonstrate that interest in and the linking of moral and linguistic concerns permeated Wittgenstein's Viennese intellectual milieu and influenced him well before he met Russell and Frege.

20. "The whole sense of the book might be summed up in the following words: what can be said at all can be said clearly, and what we cannot talk about we must pass over in silence." T, p. 3. "It must set limits to what can be thought; and, in doing so, to what cannot be thought." T, 4.114; "It will signify what cannot be said, by presenting clearly what can be said." T, 4.115. (References to many of Wittgenstein's works are made according to numbers assigned to various sections by him. I follow this convention here.)

21. T, p. 3.

22. T, 3.1. The quest for the essence of logic becomes the quest for the essence of language because thought is encased in propositions. "Thus the aim of the book is to draw a limit to thought, or rather—not to thought, but to the expression of thoughts: for in order to be able to draw a limit to thought, we should have to find both sides of the limit thinkable (i.e., we should have to think what cannot be thought). It will therefore only be in language that the limit can be drawn, and what lies on the other side of the limit will simply be nonsense." T, p. 3. One notes the Kantian flavor of this solution to philosophy's problems and yet that it is radically non-Kantian in seeking to draw the limits not to thought but to its linguistic medium.

23. NB, p. 39: "My whole task consists in explaining the nature of the proposition. That is to say, in giving the nature of all facts, whose picture the proposition is."

24. NB, p. 53; Note also T, 5.4541. Here again we find the

conviction that there must be an a priori system for appeal.

25. There is no point here in rehearsing the details of the logical problems of analysis, description and necessity which actually expressed this concern. Wittgenstein was attempting to improve on the analysis of Russell and Whithead in Principia Mathematica by developing a refined notion of the essential constant—the general form—of the proposition. For a review of the particular issues vis à vis the Principia see Kenny, Wittgenstein, pp. 43-53.

26. NB, p. 3; T, 4.0312: "The possibility of propositions is based on the principle that objects have signs as their representatives."

27. The picture theory of the proposition holds as well for thought. After all, "a thought is a proposition with a sense" (T, 4) and "a logical picture of facts is a thought" (T, 3). "The totality of true thoughts is a picture of the world" (T, 3.01). Both the totality of thought and the totality of language provide pictures of the entire world.

28. NB, p. 7. The picture theory has its beginning here: "If the right-hand figure in this picture represents the man A, and the left-hand one stands for the man B, then the whole might assert, e.g., "A is fencing with B." The proposition in picture writing can be true and false. It has a sense independent of its truth or falsehood. It must be possible to demonstrate everything essential by considering this case."

29. T, 4.01.

30. Kenny, Wittgenstein, pp. 4-5.

31. T, 4.002.

32. T, 4.011.

33. T, 4.22.

34. T, 3.26.

35. T, 3.203.

36. T, 4.0311. "In a picture the elements of the picture are the representatives of objects" (T, 2.131).

37. T, 2.021; 2.02.

38. T, 2.024-2.027.

39. T, 2.0271. Wittgenstein provides an excellent illustration in PI, 39: "The word 'Excalibur,' say, is a proper name in the ordinary sense.

The sword Excalibur consists of parts combined in a particular way. If they are combined differently Excalibur does not exist. But it is clear that the sentence 'Excalibur has a sharp blade' makes <u>sense</u> whether Excalibur is still whole or is broken up. But if 'Excalibur' is the name of an object, this object no longer exists when Excalibur is broken in pieces; and as no object would then correspond to the name it would have no meaning. But then the sentence 'Excalibur has a sharp blade' would contain a word that had no meaning, and hence the sentence would be nonsense. But it does make sense; so there must always be something corresponding to the words of which it consists. So the word 'excalibur' must disappear when the sense is analyzed and its place be taken by words which name simples. It will be reasonable to call these words the real names."

40. <u>NB</u>, p. 60. "I asked Wittgenstein whether, when he wrote the <u>Tractatus</u>, he had ever decided upon anything as an example of a 'simple object.' His reply was that at that time his thought had been that he was a <u>logician</u>; and that it was not his business, as a logician, to try to decide whether this thing or that was a simple thing or a complex thing, that being a purely <u>empirical</u> matter!" Malcolm, <u>Memoir</u>, p. 86. Confidence in the a priori method led him to overlook such difficulties. See also <u>NB</u>, p. 61.

41. <u>T</u>, 2.14.

42. As in the earlier example of "my fork is to the left of my knife," where the spatial relation of the words mirrored the spatial relation of the fork and knife. In the same manner there is a common form among, e.g., the notes of a musical score, the modulations of the singer's voice, and the grooves of her phonograph record. Logical form is needed if picturing is to be more than just going proxy for objects. It adds a definiteness to their arrangement.

43. <u>T</u>, 2.18.

44. <u>T</u>, 2.131.

45. <u>T</u>, 2.15.

46. <u>T</u>, 2.201-2.225. Names, of course, do not depend on comparison with reality and are not propositions. They are not names if they do not actually name something. What can be checked against reality is the accuracy of the particular logical form which their arrangement in this elementary proposition presents. A picture is a picture whether it depicts a possible fact or a true fact.

47. <u>T</u>, 2.1515.

48. <u>T</u>, 2.1511. "A proposition communicates a situation to us, and so it must be <u>essentially</u> connected with the situation." <u>T</u>, 4.03.

49. <u>T</u>, 3.11.

50. <u>NB</u>, p. 70; see also <u>PI</u>, 358. For some discussion of this point see Kenny, <u>Wittgenstein</u>, pp. 59-60; Hallett, <u>Companion</u>, pp. 39-40 and Henry Le Roy Finch, <u>Wittgenstein--The Later Philosophy</u> (Atlantic Highlands, New Jersey: Humanities Press, 1977), pp. 12-18.

51. <u>NB</u>, pp. 67-68. Cf. <u>PR</u>, p. 63: "If you exclude the element of intention from language, its whole function then collapses."

52. This scheme too is a result of Witgenstein's reliance on an a priori deductive method. There is a certain symptomatic vagueness to his remarks on thought. The reason why the particulars of projection, etc., are not worked out is simply that the whole project is based on inferring what must obtain if propositions can indicate facts. It had to be this way certainly, and any inability to grasp the particulars of the procedure or to locate concrete examples was not serious. After all, his was an apriori philosophy to which the shifting winds of empirical data were not relevant. For example, since language is an expression of thought and thoughts too are pictures of reality, one may wonder what the corresponding simples of thought might be. It is typical that Wittgenstein did not know and did not think it philosophically important to know. "I dont't know <u>what</u> the constituents of a thought are but I know <u>that</u> it must have such constituents which correspond to the words of language. Again the kind of realtion of the constituents of thought and of the pictured fact is irrelevant. It would be a matter of psychology to find out." Wittgenstein, <u>Letters to Russell, Keynes and Moore</u>, edited with an introduction by G. H. von Wright (Ithaca: Cornell University Press, 1974), p. 72.

53. <u>T</u>, 4.06: "A proposition can be true or false only in virtue of being a picture of reality." The structure around which the world functions and is organized may be a priori but its actual arrangement within these limitations is contingent. The point is that questions of meaning are distinct from and prior to those of truth.
I do not intend to engage the dispute over Wittgenstein's supposedly inconsistent use of <u>Sachverhalt</u> (state of affairs) and <u>Tatsache</u> (fact). In my reading they are distinct but sometimes interchangeable notions, depending on whether one is pursuing meaning or truth. The sense of my usage here is, when a possible state of affairs obtains in the world it can also be called a <u>Tatsache</u>. ("Was der Fall ist, die Tatsache, ist das Bestehen von Sachverhalten." <u>T</u>, 2). At any rate this whole excursus is not pertinent to our limited purposes here. To pursue the matter see Max Black, <u>A Companion to Wittgenstein's "Tractatus"</u> (Ithaca: Cornell University Press, 1966), pp. 39-45 and Anscombe, <u>Introduction</u>, p. 30.

54. Wittgenstein, <u>Letters</u>, p. 71.

55. <u>T</u>, 4.11: "The totality of true propositions is the whole of

natural science (or the whole corpus of the natural sciences)."

56. T, 6.16-6.12.

57. T, 4.1212. See also 4.12-4.1211.

58. T, 3.221; 6.432; 6.42; 6.421.

59. T, 6.41. "Propositions can express nothing that is higher." T, 6.42. "How things are in the world is a matter of complete indifference for what is higher. God does not reveal himself in the world." T, 6.432.

60. No amount of scientific information, including a scientific philosophy, can solve the deep questions of life. The importance of this view for the Tractatus is spelled out by Wittgenstein in a letter to Ludwig von Ficker: "The book's point is an ethical one. I once meant to include in the preface a sentence which is not in fact there now but which I will write out for you here, because it will perhaps be a key to the work for you. What I meant to write, then, was this: My work consists of two parts: the one presented here plus all that I have not written. And it is precisely this second part that is the important one. My book draws limits to the sphere of the ethical from the inside as it were, and I am convinced that this is the ONLY rigorous way of drawing those limits. In short, I believe that where many others today are just gassing, I have managed in my book to put everything firmly into place by being silent about it. And for that reason, unless I am very much mistaken, the book will say a great deal that you yourself want to say. Only perhaps you won't see that it is said in the book. For now, I would recommend you to read the preface and the conclusion, because they contain the most direct expression of the point of the book." Englemann, Letters, pp. 143-44.

61. T, 7.

62. Wittgenstein, "Notes on Logic," ed. H. T. Costello, in NB, p. 93; T, 4.111.

63. T, 6.53.

64. "Philosophy aims at the logical clarification of thoughts. Philosophy is not a body of doctrine but an activity. A philosophical work consists essententially of elucidations. Philosophy does not result in 'philosophical propositions,' but rather in the clarification of propositions. Without philosophy thoughts are, as it were, cloudy and indistinct; its task is to make them clear and to give them sharp boundaries." T, 4.112.

65. T, 6.54.

66. Wittgenstein himself later saw that this earlier work was not truly methodological in the praxis-oriented sense of his later work. What

the <u>Tractatus</u> actually does is to put forth another foundational <u>theory</u>, viz., the picture theory of language.

CHAPTER FOUR
LANGUAGE AND METHOD IN THE LATER WITTGENSTEIN

The fundamental task of the Tractatus was never abandoned by Wittgenstein. Philosophy remained for him an exercise in linguistic consciousness-raising focused on the problem of meaning (that is, on the connection of thought, language and the world) and designed to remedy philosophical confusion. Elucidating the way is the philosopher's task, and that way—the way in and the way out of philosophical puzzlement—is linguistic.[1] Nevertheless, the Philosophical Investigations is in radical discontinuity with Wittgenstein's earlier period. If the continuity between the earlier and the later Wittgenstein lies in his general view of the philosophical task, the discontinuity lies in Wittgenstein's new approach to this task: the method of a priori analysis is to be abandoned in favor of the a posteriori method of description. The aim of philosophy is "to show the fly out of the fly-bottle."[2] The limits-to language are no longer set by an analysis of the necessary and essential limits-of language. Rather it is enough for philosophy to note linguistic use and bring it to consciousness. No particular linguistic behavior is demanded, actual linguistic behavior is simply noted. The wish for a clear, distinct, universal and permanent border between meaningfulness and meaninglessness vanishes before the tangled, meandering filigree of actual usage. The Tractatus was essentialist in its view of language: it presumed that universal terms such as "language" and "proposition" must operate by designating certain fixed essences. This notion is destroyed in the Investigations: taking a look at our working language disabuses the author and his readers of essentialism and undermines atomism or any other a priori harness on meaning. Both early and late, Wittgenstein viewed philosophy as an activity. He saw his writings as an elucidation of problems: once those writings had brought the reader to "see the world aright" they themselves could be discarded. He remained convinced of the linguistic nature of this task. But what did change was his understanding of the method proper to its accomplishment. In his later period deduction gives way to observation, prescription is replaced by description. Wittgenstein is still intent on the need to show us that which cannot fruitfully be said, but his understanding of this project has shifted significantly. Meaning is still key, but the early essentialism and atomism have become a problem, not a solution.

For Ludwig Wittgenstein the source of philosophical problems is the bewitchment of our minds by language. This confusion arises when the engine of language is "idling" rather than when it is doing its work.[3] In the Philosophical Investigations this idling is not a straying from the one foundation of all language as defined by a Tractarian theory. This standard is rejected and the unity of a theory is replaced by the diversity of use. "Philosophical problems arise when language goes on holiday."[4] The antidote is to bring words back to their home, to see them at work in their habitual context and usage. This is not an attempt to ban all extraordinary philosophical usage. Nothing could be less Wittgensteinian. It is a warning to recall the baggage, the "natural history," the word will bring with it into its new context.[5] Failure to do so can be a source of confusion. Awareness of the working linguistic facts can put a new light on various philosophical puzzles. In this way a problematic may be dissolved rather than solved. This does not require a special knowledge of the theoretical structure of all language, but rather is simply a recalling of concrete, trivial facts about our ordinary use of our language. The vanishing of philosophical problems is directly related to this sort of linguistic attentiveness.

The major danger in philosophy has been seen as the failure to give meaning to certain signs in one's propositions. Establishing meaning was a function of linking names and objects in a picturing relationship. But later Wittgenstein began to wonder if this view of meaning squared with the actual way in which we use language. Could the elucidations of a Tractatus or an Investigations be judged nonsensical in se? Or is this determined by how they are used? What Wittgenstein rejected was not his earlier view of the general task of philosophy, but a particular solution for that task, viz., theory of meaning and truth which supposed that language functions as an exact calculus mirroring the exact structure of the world.[6] For the later Wittgenstein, philosophy remained fundamentally linguistic and methodological, but these concerns were no longer seen in the light of strict definition and a priori structure.

Although it would not be possible or useful to give a systematic and substantive account of this Wittgensteinian shift, still one can note some of the features of this horizon. Awareness of the Tractatus type of philosophizing is important background. For the later Wittgenstein, philosophical problems are often the result of our being misled by our language. "When words in our ordinary language have prima facie analogous grammars we are inclined to try to interpret them analogously; i.e., we try to make the analogy hold throughout."[7] Asking about the meaning of the words at hand is therefore a good safeguard for the inquiring philosopher. As additional bearings for negotiating the later Wittgenstein, let us select two characteristic themes of his later work: his exhortation to look rather than to think and his pedagogical use of the language-game. These points are not in any sense theses of Wittgenstein's, but rather are typical of the sort of directions he offers to the disoriented philosopher. Admonitions such as "don't think, but look!"[8] and the concomitant employment of language-games are ways of helping philosophers orient the linguistic map they so badly need to consult. Looking and attending to "games" are ways of responding to the possibility that some philosophical problems are conceptual problems. These three themes are typical of the later Wittgenstein. His perspective includes, among other things, an invitation to take a look, a confrontation with language-games, and a controlling suspicion that the roots of confusion may be conceptual. Understanding these pointers can help bring into focus what is going on in the Philosophical Investigations. While there is no checklist of essential Wittgensteinian dogmas, a discussion of some of the motifs of his later work may provide a good sense of his direction.

Taking a Look

The demand to look and not to let thinking take the place of looking is an admonition to avoid the method of theoretical inference, presupposition, and prescription so perfected in the Tractatus. With this latter method one need not attend to the multiplicity of cases but rather can determine in advance what must always be the case. As Wittgenstein knew so well, partiality to this approach is a result of the philosopher's craving for generality and his infatuation with the possibility of a scientific philosophy.[9] This assimilation of the method of philosophy to the method of science can be thought of, for Wittgenstein, as a continuous search for similarities and the companion tendency to supress or dismiss differences. In the natural sciences one reduces phenomena to a small number of basic laws. In mathematics one developes a generalization to unify several diverse topics. Perhaps in philosophy too one may seek to reduce and generalize the differences of various data in terms of a single universal, simple structure that is deduced from similarities. But this craving encourages the supposition that if one often uses the same word for various entities then there must be some sort of essence or exemplar common to each particular instance. For example, one understands all the various things which count as a leaf because one has formed some sort of a standard or picture of "leaf" which abstracts from and is not identical to any particular leaf. This conclusion is deduced; it is not the result of limiting oneself to description of actual linguistic behavior. Such a move is typical of the way in which philosophical presumptions about language give birth to new metaphysical or epistemological entities.

> Philosophers constantly see the method of science before their eyes, and are irresistibly tempted to ask and answer questions in the way science does. This tendency is the real source of metaphysics, and leads the philosopher into complete darkness.[10]

But what does philosphy do if it is not in this sense scientific? How does one avoid "complete darkness" and become instead a philosopher of the light?

The later Wittgenstein advises us simply to begin to look. We must refuse to subjugate what we see is the case to what we think ought to be the case. We must note the irreducible diversity which our bias toward simplification urges us to overlook. It is philosophy's business to describe what is there. It does not generate new entities by reducing concrete cases to their supposed similarities; it relishes differences. It is true that philosophy must remedy its own confusion, but to be scientific is not the solution. "I want to say here that it can never be our job to reduce anything to anything, or to explain anything. Philosophy is really 'purely descriptive.'"[11] There is to be a shift in focus, then, from abstract similarities to concrete differences. This method of description may prove much more useful in untangling philosophical knots.

The Tractatus was a paradigmatic attempt to develop a generalized structure of the world and to found a scientific philosophy. The starting point was linguistic. The procedure was to seek, by analysis, the a priori, general form of all propositions, of all language and finally of the world. Having assumed that such a search could be fruitful, young Wittgenstein naturally found that it was. He claimed to have discovered the structure of that logical space which determines the conditions for the possibility of all facts of experience. By analyzing discourse he arrived at the structure of reality which that discourse must reflect. The point of departure was the empirical phenomenon of language, but this phenomenon was viewed as merely superficial. The aim was to locate the essence hidden within it. Concrete differences withered in the face of dogmatic demands. There must be an essence at work here.

> . . . For they see in the essence, not something that already lies open to view and that becomes surveyable by a rearrangement, but something that lies beneath the surface. Something that lies within, which we see when we look into the thing, and which an analysis digs out.
> 'The essence is hidden from us:' this is the form our problem now assumes. We ask: "What is language?," "What is a proposition?" And the answer to these questions is to be given once for all; and independently of any future experience.[12]

What was sought was something invisible to be posited by deduction or induction rather than discovered by the common sense empiricism of observation. Wittgenstein summarizes the thrust of his earlier method when he remarks, "We feel as if we had to penetrate phenomena."[13]

If the world had a structure a priori, philosophy could be of great help by laying bare that skeleton and holding it high as the standard of meaningfulness. The project was founded on the supposition that in order to work, language must picture the world. From this Wittgenstein inferred the necessity of an essential and precise parallelism of words and things. His hard thinking about propositions and their relation to the world was, from first to last, a priori in orientation. Logic was seen as presenting

> . . . an order, in fact the a priori order of the world: that is, the order of possibilities, which must be common to both world and thought. But this order, it seems, must be utterly simple. It is prior to all experience, must run through all experience; no empirical cloudiness or uncertainty can be allowed to affect it--it must rather be of the purest crystal.[14]

This pure, non-empirical crystal was to be the foundation for philosophical certainty. Hence Wittgenstein confesses that in the Tractatus "what is peculiar, profound, essential in our investigations, resides in its trying to grasp the incomparable essence of language."[15] This focus on essence also meant that particular concrete cases were of minor significance; they were simply instances of that great structure which the philosophical x-ray of analysis had exposed.[16] The a priori method of analysis searches for essence and similarity in order to bring a clarity that it seemed was unavailable in the contingent diversity presented by simple description. The underlying and generalized "essence of language" was of paramount importance. All else was secondary and derivative. The later Wittgenstein was to pull this perspective inside out.

That there was an essential structure was an intuition Wittgenstein later abandoned. In the Investigations the particular case becomes very important and the "essence of language" illusory.[17] The Tractatus view is reversed: its picture of language and meaning was the result of supposing what had to be and not of looking at what actually was. The disappearance of a determinative a priori structure of the world and language was a direct result of simply ceasing to presume it. The shift from the Tractarian standpoint to that of the Philosophical Investigations, from an analytical to an empirical linguistic philosophy, is the shift from the method of definition to that of description. On Moritz Schlick's copy of the Tractatus Wittgenstein wrote: "Every one of these sentences is the expression of an illness." As we have seen this illness consisted in the tendency to seek the simple and unique essence of language and the world and to fix these by definition. Once these foundations are laid bare, it became possible to distinguish that which can be said (scientific meaning) from the meaningless pseudo-propositions of metaphysics. This was clarity. The search for such a foundation was, of course, the result of a fascination with the universal generalizations of scientific theory and the intuition that essences must be involved. Accordingly, the Tractatus was able to put forth a very definite picture of the foundations for inquiry.

> Thought, language, now appear to us as the unique correlate, picture, of the world, stand in line one behind the other, each equivalent to each.[18]

This illusory order is an illness, a bewitchment, to which the philosopher often succumbs. It is the result of his craving for generality and of his tendency to feel that he must penetrate phenomena. The foregoing diagnosis calls forth a form of linguistic therapy from the attending philosopher. "The philosopher's treatment of a question is like the treatment of an illness."[19] It is the nature of the illness which dictates the style and approach of the Philosophical Investigations.

"What is your aim in philosophy?—to show the fly the way out of the fly-bottle."[20] The philosopher is like the fly who has been lured into this trap: she continues to fly upward and to bang into the invisible wall of the bottle. Fixing her gaze on the clear sky above, she ignores the exit route below her. So it is that an enclosure with a hole in it is quite a good jail if the prisoner systematically fails to notice the opening. The Tractatus syndrome is seductive; since we do know what we mean, our language, however vague it appears, must be a good mirror. The result of Wittgenstein's own failure to really look at language was the development of a logical atomism to explain the essential mirroring activity of language. We are all susceptible to such eisegesis.[21] In the end, the source of our vexation and constraint is our own vision. What we see is not the self-evident manifestation of essence but rather a specter created for us by our method. In Wittgenstein's atomism "the crystalline purity of logic was, of course, not a result of investigation; it was a requirement."[22] But there are other ways to make the same mistake. Other philosophies can be guilty, mutatis mutandis, of the same general methodological oversight. They can set a heuristic whose terms are dictated by a craving for generality, fascination with similarity, and a disdain for the particular case. The demands which are read into our horizon go as unnoticed as the glasses on our nose; they are as transparent—and as frustrating—as the walls of a fly-bottle. The only way out for the poor confused fly is to stop presuming he knows the way and to begin looking at the bottle very carefully.

If we are to find our way out, we must attend to language as it is rather than as we would like it. This means getting clear on the actual functions of words in their contexts.[23] "A philosophical problem has the form: 'I don't know my way about.'" The solution is to get a feel for the linguistic terrain. Wittgenstein is very explicit about this as the purpose of his Investigations.

> The philosophical remarks in this book are, as it were, a number of sketches of landcapes which were made in the course of these long and involved journeyings.
> The same or almost the same points were always being approached afresh from different directions, and new sketches made. Very many of these were badly drawn or uncharacteristic, marked by all the defects of a weak draughtsman. And when there were rejected a number of tolerable ones were left, which now had to be arranged and sometimes cut down, so that if you looked at them you could get a picture of the landscape. Thus this book is really only an album.[24]

Getting lost in language is the problem. We need to get our bearings. We do this by tracking back and forth over our language from a number of slightly different philosophical angles until the over-all use of a word in our language is clear. The records of these journeyings are just close accounts of particular bits of the jungle. When put together these snapshots do not form an exact and complete picture of every inch of language. Rather they provide the sort of general feel one gets from looking through an album. And this is just the sort of "picture of the landscape" we need. Not the darkness of a complete and opaque theoretical account but the light cast on the whole by a single well-selected example.

Language is the medium of our investigations. In order to get a clearer understanding of, for example, thinking or willing, we must begin to look at actual linguistic practice. We must attend to the language we have and the ways we actually use it. Why force one use to be the model for all uses? Why not take a look? The neat, orderly, scientific suburbs of language are not to be confused with the tangled streets of the ancient city.[25] Philosophical confusion can result from captivation by a single picture of all meaning. "A <u>picture</u> held us captive. And we could not get outside of it, for it lay in our language and language seemed to repeat it to us inexorably."[26] But is that picture really present there? Philosophy must beware of analysis, of its tendency to feel it must penetrate rather than observe phenomena, of the danger that a wish will overcome the reality. Whatever "essence" of language there is can be found not in the hidden depths of language but right on its surface, for "all the facts that concern us lie open before us."[27] There is no need of theoretical explanations. The first move is to look, not to think.

Thus the hold of a picture is broken. The picture of how language must be (a priori) can only be smashed by looking at how it is (a posteriori).

> Philosophy simply puts everything before us, and neither explains nor deduces anything.--Since everything lies open to view there is nothing to explain. For what is hidden, for example, is of no interest to us.[28]

The problem is a failure to look at the actual language involved and the solution is simply to look. "A main source of our failure to understand is that we do not <u>command</u> a <u>clear</u> <u>view</u> of the use of our words."[29] The way to attain this view is by close attention to particular examples which eschews our blinding bias; one must resist the temptation to shave off the differences between uses in the interest of assembling a universal essence. The penultimate focus of this investigation may be on examples; however its final goal is not a linguistic anatomy but the curing of an illness through the shifting of one's methodological horizon. The validation of this escape from "foundations" lies in its actual dissolution of real philosophical problems.

Language-Games

The problem is not having a clear view of our language and the solution is description. But how are we to bring our language to consciousness? What is a method through which we can describe the linguistic landscape? Wittgenstein's reconnaissance takes the characteristic shape of what he calls the remark (<u>Bermerkung</u>).³⁰ A remark is an occasion for linguistic awareness. They may be sentences or paragraphs and may take the form of questions, exhortations, cases, reactions, stories, or even intentionally false statements. The <u>Philosophical Investigations</u> is a concatenation of philosophical remarks with direction and thematic organization but without any kind of systematic closure.³¹ Its purpose is to provide an album that will give us a feel for our linguistic surroundings. Wittgenstein's "snapshots" bring the imagination to bear on particular cases. He prods us into linguistic self-reflection. Wittgenstein's remarks seldom leave us as they found us.

The use of remarks is a well-known and well-calculated facet of Wittgenstein's style. The most famous type of remark is probably the language-game. The language-game, for Wittgenstein, is both a metaphor for a linguistic fact and a tool for highlighting that fact.

One of the key insights of Wittgenstein's descriptive method is that in language we play games with words. The term "language-game" is used to remind us of this fact and of its implications for meaning. How words mean is a function of the particular game at hand. Games do have rules but these rules shift with the game. This interest in actual use--in the game being played--replaces the axiom that all use must be the same, that there is only one game played by meaningful language. Rather, if we want to find the meaning we are to look for the use.

> For a <u>large</u> class of cases--though not for all--in which we employ the word "meaning" it can be defined thus: the meaning of a word is its use in the language.³²

The uses of language are various: obeying and giving orders, describing the appearance of objects, telling jokes, cursing, praying, etc. To understand a word is to be prepared for one of its uses. Understanding the rules for these various uses means backing up and looking at the socio-linguistic context. Simply having the vocabulary is not enough. One must ask, what game is being played here? By referring to language as a game Wittgenstein keeps before us the wider horizon for meaning and stresses that the speaking of a language is a practice within a whole stream of life, language and culture. "I shall also call the whole, consisting of language and the actions into which it is woven, the 'language-game.'"³³ Language and our forms of life weave a tapestry, and the meaning of that tapestry disappears if they are unravelled. "Only in the stream of thought and life do words have meaning."³⁴

But attention to the fact of language-games can be focused by actually playing through particular games. The language-game is also a major tool of the later Wittgenstein. A theory can be looked at by enfleshing it in a faithfully drawn concrete instance and operating a descriptive interrogation. The point is to drive the philosopher to look at what is quite describable: ordinary simple cases. From these one can draw implications for more complex uses. All of this is done as a corrective to the habit of presuming the use a priori. "One cannot guess how a word functions. One has to look at its uses and learn from that."[35] Looking is facilitated by an imaginative simplification of our complex language and language-games into striking examples capable of presenting the conceptual landscape. These cases provide grist for Wittgenstein's philosophical remarks. "It disperses the fog to study the phenomena of language in primitive kinds of application in which one can command a clear view of the aim and functioning of the words."[36]

> If we want to study the problems of truth and falsehood, of the agreement and disagreement of propositions with reality, of the nature of assertion, assumption, and question, we shall with great advantage look at primitive forms of language in which these forms of thinking appear without the confusing background of highly complicated processes of thought. When we look at such simple forms of language the mental mist which seems to enshroud our ordinary use of language disappears. We see activities, reactions, which are clear-cut and transparent. On the other hand we recognize in these simple processes forms of language not separated by a break from our more complicated ones.[37]

These example cases, whether complex or simplified, display the rules of the games played and the importance of the total context. They are language-games selected or created by Wittgenstein to highlight the reality and function of the language-game. The point of all this, of course, is to shed some light on specific philosophical problems. The method is a method of examples. Samples are Wittgenstein's way of recalling the first-hand experience and familiarity he needs to survey the linguistic geography.[38] The recalling of this geography is an attempt to recollect the contours which shape philosophical exploration.

Effecting this consciousness of language-games is the task of Wittgenstein's remarks. They do not present us with new data but merely remind us of certain facts about our use of language which we have always known but which we do not need to reflect upon until we get lost in the linguistic manipulations of philosophy (or theology or Freudian psychology or whatever). It is in this sense that "The work of the philosopher consists in assembling reminders for a particular purpose."[39] The album of Philosophical Investigations is a set of reminders and remarks. These cases, questions, and exhortations make us look for the use, and this search for use makes us look to the wider socio-linguistic context of our language. This is how philosophical problems are solved.

The descriptive method demands that one focus on the observable use of a word before he begins to presume how it means. Thus the description of a word's ordinary use is the antidote to metaphysics and analysis: it destroys the theory that meaning requires a correlation of thought, word and language. "Here the word, there the meaning. The money and the cow you buy with it."[40] In fact when one looks at use one finds that meaning is not simply given by an object—whether one places that object in the world, or in the mind or locates it as some process, feeling or experience accompanying the word. Rather we find that language has no one universal structure of meaning, that instead words are like tools in a toolbox: they are characterized by their uses. There is no single essential function for all words just as here is no single function for all tools.[41] Words may look alike but not have the same functions. Think of the cabin of a locomotive with all of the various handles.

> We see handles all looking more or less alike. (Naturally, since they are all supposed to be handled.) But one is the handle of a crank which can be moved continuosly (it regulates the opening of a valve); another is the handle of a switch, which has only two effective positions, it is either off or on; a third is the handle of a brake-lever; the harder one pulls on it, the harder it brakes; a fourth, the handle of a pump: it has an effect only so long as it is moved to and fro.[42]

Words do not have any one limited function but our own questions about meaning make us think so. We set a false heuristic when we ask "<u>What</u> is meaning?" Such questions about the meaning of a word (or of truth, beauty, etc.) "produce in us a mental cramp. We feel that we can't point to anything in reply to them and yet ought to point to something. (We are up against one of the great sources of philosophical bewilderment: a substantive makes us look for a thing that corresponds to it.)"[43] A cure for this illness is to replace the question "what is the meaning?" with the question "what is an explanation of meaning?" Decsription of use cures us of this temptation to look for an object which defines the word and turns us instead to the linguistic and social context.

Describing the behavior of our words has both positive and negative import for the question of meaning: it highlights the actual role of use in meaning while it points up a fatal flaw in any universal, essentialist theory of meaning. Two famous examples of this descriptive procedure and critique are Wittgenstein's remarks on the word "game" in the <u>Investigations</u> and his use of the method of "tove" in the <u>Blue Book</u>.

Wittgenstein's treatment of the concept "game" is a good example of the way in which a careful look at a particular case can demolish a towering theoretical edifice. His description of the uses of "game" makes rather untenable the presumption that all words mean by virtue of correlation with a referent. Do concepts have fixed essences to hook into the world? Wittgenstein is content with a modest interrogation of a word:

is there an essence discernable amid all of the various applications of the word "game?" This simple investigation will display the value of attention to the particular case. For a look at just one concept could bring our language into view and end the fascination with essentialism. If all language is supposed to work in the same way, essential linguistic feature mirroring essential ontological feature, then any exception to this universal rule negates it.

The word "game" is used of many different things on many different occasions. Yet according to analytical method there is present among these variations an isolable constant peculiar to this and only this word. Will a descriptive method see this too? Is there an essence to "game," some simple linguistic point at which this word can be linked with its singular counterpart in the world? A look at the actual behavior of the word in our language offers little support for this theoretical vision.

> Consider for example the proceedings that we call "games." I mean board-games, card-games, ball-games, Olympic games, and so on. What is common to them all? Don't say: "There must be something common, or they would not be called 'games'"--but look and see whether there is anything at all.—For if you look at them you will not see something that is common to all, but similarities, relationships, and whole series of them at that. To repeat: don't think, but look!—Look for example at board-games, with their multifarious relationships. Now pass to card-games; here you find many correspondences with the first group, but many common features drop out, and others appear. When we pass next to ball-games, much that is common is retained, but much is lost. Are they all "amusing?" Compare chess with naughts and crosses. Or is there always winning and losing; but when a child throws his ball at the wall and catches it again, this feature has disappeared. Look at the parts played by skill and luck; and at the difference between skill in chess and skill in tennis. Think now of games like ring-a-ring-a-roses; here is the element of amusement, but how many other characteristic features have disappeared! And we can go through the many, many other groups of games in the same way; can see how similarities crop up and disappear.
> And the result of this examination is: we see a complicated network of similarities overlapping and criss-crossing: sometimes overall similarities, sometimes similarities of detail.[44]

I can think of no better expression to characterize

these similarities than "family resemblances"; for the various resemblances between members of a family: build, features, colour of eyes, gait, temperament, etc., etc., overlay and criss-cross in the same way--and I shall say: "games" form a family.[45]

A "family resemblance" does not have the identity of an essence. Wittgenstein's descriptive inquiry has shown no invariable core in the word "game." That is just not part of the natural linguistic history of the world. In this sample there is no fixed and invariant essence to line up with reality. One may select various exact meanings in context, but no one meaning necessarily subsists. This means that, from the concept's side, the idea of a single, universal, mirroring structure for the meaning of all language is not workable. The observed differences have been fatal. Of course the differing uses do overlap and do bear some resemblance to each other, but their similarity is found to be more like the indefinable and shifting similarity among the members of a family than a precise, sharp and constant essence. A description of actual uses discovers only the vague likeness of a family resemblance. And this cannot be grapsed outside the context of use and usage.

Language is more like a game than a steady mirror. This game is very important for understanding meaning. Still, there have been those who argued or acted as if the meaning of a word was <u>solely</u> a function of its "reaching out to the world." The tendency to overlook language as a source in the explanation of meaning runs deep.

A case which sheds a good deal of light on this dimension of the problem of meaning is the attack on completely a-linguistic ostensive definition which begins the <u>Blue Book</u>.[46] Recall that on one theory the meaning of a word is only penultimately verbal. Words can be explained and interpreted by other words (as in analysis) only up to a point. Ultimately a word's definition is ostensive: one hooks up the word and its meaning by a sort of Adamic naming. On the most basic level the meaning of words is a function of pointing to the object and saying its companion word: "Tisch, Fenster, etc." But can we really conclude that the meaning is what is pointed to? There is first some trouble over what one might be pointing at when words like "no," "yet," "how," or "freedom" come forth. Then there is the problem of whether or not pointing is an effective guarantor of meaning anyway. The problem is that ostensive definition can be misunderstood. If ostensive definition can be misunderstood, then perhaps it is not the final control on meaning. Wittgenstein asks us to imagine explaining the word "tove" by pointing to a pencil and saying "this is tove." The ostensive definition "this is tove" can be interpreted in various ways. For example, the words and gesture may mean "this is a pencil," "this is round," "this is wood," "this is one," "this is hard," "this is yellow," etc. The definition can always be misunderstood and is unclear. (Think of the problems involved in a literal translation of German idioms.) But if spoken within a certain context and to persons trained in the usage of language, the meaning is quite exact and clear. If I know we are talking about various colors, then when you say "this is tove" I know with which feature of the object you link the word. Likewise there is no vagueness once I realize we are concerned with distinguishing a <u>Bleistift</u> from a <u>Kugelschreiber</u>. Ostensive definition alone is not sufficient for clarity. One only understands ostensive definition when one is aware of its wider context in our life and language.[47] The ground of understanding language is knowing how the language is used and grasping the context of this particular usage.

Wittgenstein's new approach takes the form of an ad hoc interrogation of actual linguistic samples done in a way faithful to the demand to look and a wary of theory and definition. And much is learned, for example, by a short study of "game" or "tove." Simple cases viewed in a particular light can surface the types of moves behind more complex cases. One is provided with an example of how the method of observation deflates that of analysis, deduction, and universal generalization. Looking at the games we play with words brings home to us the importance and variation of use. It cripples the persistent inclination to view language as a polished schema reflecting the world. It circumvents the search for foundations as a search for privileged representations or metaphysical structures. Meaning is rooted in something far more obvious and homey.

Meaning seems to be a function of use in a context. Meaning is not established by merely pointing to some object but emerges in the weave of particular use and common usage. There is evidence that the presence of a linguistic essence cannot be presumed for all words and that even if such an essence were possible, simply pointing to its "counterpart" in the world would not be equivalent to understanding its meaning.

This is not to say that meaning cannot be set by definition. It can. But one must be aware that definition is at work and not confuse its accomplishments with those of an empirical investigation of the world. A sharply defined term is not equivalent to a reliable reflection of nature. A new definition unnoticed can confuse the unwary reader and the forgetful writer. Definitions have life and breath and being only in a concrete socio-linguistic constellation. Thus, it seems fruitful for the working philosopher (or theologian) to separate and distinguish the conceptual from the metaphysical. Looking at language-games shifts the horizon for inquiry and as the horizon shifts what comes into view is "grammar."

<u>Foundational Investigations: Conceptual Investigations</u>

The turn to grammar represents the primary outcome of the later Wittgenstein's descriptive method. If using language is like playing a game, then discovering the grammar at work is like discovering the rules of the game. A certain grammar is implicit in our use of language much as the rules for a game are implicit in the game; they can be read off of it. This grammar is not that schoolboy subject concerned with syntax and phonetic elements but rather attends to the equally pervasive and elementary rules for the use of a word both in our culture and at play in specific contexts. It is a matter of the ordinary linguistic practice which guides our use; it is a matter of the natural history of a word. For example, the phrase "I believe...falsely" is in good English grammar, but is a manifest violation of the conceptual grammar to which Wittgenstein would have us attend. The ordinary logic of the word "believe" is such that in certain circumstances one cannot apply the adverb "falsely" to it. "If there were a verb meaning 'to believe falsely,' it would not have any significant first person present indicative."[48] It is just not part of the way we commonly behave with the word. Wittgenstein turns our attention to this conceptual grammar constantly. Another typical remark is "A man can pretend to be unconscious; but conscious?"[49] Again we suddenly realize that we just do not use the words "conscious" and "pretend" in that way. There are times when we must recall this wider grammatical context in order to avoid confusion in philosophy. It is not a grammar to be fixed or recorded forever; there is too much variety in its family of uses for that. This grammar is a matrix of roles for use discovered by observation of what we do and not prescribed by analysis of what we ought to do. Wittgenstein's remarks force us to describe the linguistic terrain in such a way as to highlight its grammatical contours.

One's horizon, then, must be marked by the realization that "only in the stream of thought and life do words have meaning."[50] So for example, "The concept of pain is characterized by its particular function in our life. Only surrounded by certain normal manifestations of life is there such a thing as an expression of pain."[51] To ignore this is to invite a confusion of grammars and knots in our understanding. This confusion is a major hazard of philosophical thinking. We tend to look only at the form of the words and not at the use made of the form of the words.[52] "We remain unconscious of the prodigious diversity of all the everyday language-games because the clothing of our language makes everything alike."[53] Words appear uniform and so we tend to ignore their less obvious differences of application. We fail to distinguish the surface grammar, that is, that part of the use that presents itself immediately, that can, so to speak, be taken in by the ear, from the depth grammar, that is, the application of these words in the stream of life and language. Similarity of appearance can divert us from differences of application. "When words in our ordinary language have prima facie analogous grammars we are inclined to try to interpret them analogously, i.e., we try to make the analogy hold throughout."[54] Our craving for generality and similarity disposes us to settle for similarity in surface grammar and to ignore depth grammar. This bewitchment of our minds by the grammar of our language is a major source of our philosophical puzzlement.

In doing philosophy one tends to overlook grammar and to generate from it impossible philosophical dilemmas. The grounds and problems of philosophy are conceptual yet they are frequently construed as empirical and scientific. Metaphysical statements about the world often turn on a grammatical blind spot.

> Philosophical investigations: conceptual investigations. The essential thing about metaphysics: it obliterates the distinction between factual and conceptual investigations.[55]

Metaphysics is a consistent failure to distinguish the conceptual and the factual. To cross criteria of application in this way is to invite confusion. For a simple example of this confusion, consider these three statements:

1. Only one person can play solitaire.
2. Only one person can sit on a bench six inches wide.
3. Only one person can feel my pain.

The surface grammars are similar, but the conceptual grammars are quite different. The first impossibility is given by the grammar alone: ordinary use of the word "solitaire" is limited to a single person playing cards. The second is a physical impossibility: the available space is limited. The third is the kind of statement which philosophers tend to interpret on the model of number two, but which is really like number one. The issue in number three is grammatical, not scientific or experiential. The "can" signals a conceptual impossibility, not a physiological datum and still less a metaphysical necessity. The failure to note this grammar can balloon into complex questions of privacy, pain criteria, solipsism, etc., which purport to be questions of fact but which are—in actual linguistic fact—the result of grammatical oversight.[56]

This mixture of the factual and conceptual also occurs when one feels driven to stretch a word's usage, to be a linguistic pioneer. While there is no problem with adopting an uncommon use for certain words, there is a danger that one will forget to post this divergence from ordinary meaning. The result may be the confusion of grammatical invention with empirical discovery and the consequent creation of a metaphysical quandary. For example, someone may find it useful to begin to speak of a certain stage of not-yet-painful tooth decay as "unconscious toothache" and to therefore talk about having a toothache but not knowing it. There is nothing wrong with this; it is just a new terminology and can easily be translated back into ordinary language. But it does alter the grammar of the word "to know" and to the extent that this alternation goes unnoticed, integration of this new use may begin to conjure up many old uses and analogies. Suddenly one is puzzled.

> Thus, by the expression "unconscious toothache" you may either be misled into thinking that a stupendous discovery has been made, a discovery which in a sense altogether bewilders our understanding; or else you may be extremely puzzled by the expression (the puzzlement of philosophy) and perhaps ask such a question as "How is unconscious toothache possible?" You may

then be tempted to deny the possibility of unconscious toothache, but the scientist will tell you that it is a proved fact that there is such a thing, and he will say it like a man who is destroying a common prejudice. He will say: "Surely it's quite simple; there are other things which you don't know of, and there can also be toothache which you don't know of. It is just a new discovery." You won't be satisfied, but you won't know what to answer.[57]

The solution is to attend to the grammar, to ask how "to know" is used in this case and how it is used in other cases and how far the analogy between these cases can be taken. Again, attention to the grammar of the case at hand avoids the confusion of the conceptual and the factual.[58]

The confusion of the grammatical with the experiential leads philosophers to say many things, including metaphysical things. The striking discoveries of metaphysics are often founded not on new facts about the world but on equivocation in our language. Both science and philosophy may put the question "quid sit" but the criteria for a proper answer differ in the extreme. To make one do duty for the other is to restrain them both. Factual investigations are not to be confused with conceptual investigations. Science does the job of science in a scientific manner. Philosophical investigations are conceptual investigations. "The fundamental thing expressed grammatically; what about the sentence 'One cannot step into the same river twice?'"[59] New information about the deep structure of the world or a classic conceptual problem?

Overlooking the jobs done by our language is a serious and counterproductive misstep. The tasks which metaphysical analysis sets itself are not within its competency. "Like everything the harmony between thought and reality is to be found in the grammar of the language."[60]

These then are the general lines of Wittgenstein's new method. The essential point of departure is that "philosophy, as we use the word, is a fight against the fascination which forms of expression exert upon us."[61] Dissolving real philosophical problems by creating attentiveness to language is the job of his philosophical investigations. Wittgenstein asks questions to get his readers to look at a particularly vital spot as this is presented in simple cases formulated to display the depth grammar of our words. In this way we can look at language and avoid the trap of theory. Insight comes from the examination of particular cases which show the grammar governing the possibility of various phenomena. The confusion of the conceptual and the factual is avoided. The key is to look, to observe linguistic behavior. This is done by questions and cases--language-games--which highlight the grammar. The three watchwords of Wittgenstein's linguistic therapy are look, language-game, and grammar.

Language and Method

Wittgenstein's new method is a method of models and concrete examples. Its aim is not to be a new system but to occasion a personal conversion to a framework for understanding philosophical problems. This new horizon is linguistic and radical. It is foundational in a new and very different sense of the word. It does not look at language from some sort of privileged epistemological or metaphysical ground, but simply in order to be aware of its influence.[62] Philosophical problems which seemed to be factual now appear as conceptual. Furthermore, resolving these conceptual problems requires a conscious recollection of the ordinary workings of language. But acquiring linguistic common sense remains difficult because philosophers, in striving to be scientific, tend to ignore the role of depth grammar in philosophical inquiry and to focus instead on the quasi-factual contributions of metaphysical analysis. For this reason Wittgenstein's project is ongoing and therapeutic.

> And we may not advance any kind of theory. There must not be anything hypothetical in our considerations. We must do away with all <u>explanation</u>, and description alone must take its place. And this description gets its light, that is to say its purpose, from the philosophical problems. These are, of course, not empirical problems; they are solved, rather, by looking into the workings of our language, and that in such a way as to make us recognize those workings: <u>in despite of</u> an urge to misunderstand them. The problems are solved, not by giving new information, but by arranging what we have always known. Philosophy is a battle against the bewitchment of our intelligence by means of language.[63]

The <u>Philosophical Investigations</u> can be seen as a vaccine used when and where needed in order to build up in us an immunity to infectious grammatical oversight. The remedy is administered in discrete doses of description, each tailored to place particular issues in the light of their general socio-linguistic context. The result is a new perspective on philosophical problems. It is this higher perspective which is the essence of Wittgenstein's method. "It is as if one had altered the adjustment of a microscope. One did not see before what is now in focus."[64] This shift is a shift in horizon which brings the everyday workings of our language into view. The knots tied, for example, by a Tractarian method, are dissolved in the methodic shift of the <u>Philosophical Investigations</u>.

The shift in method also turns a new light on old issues. The crucial and continuous thread of Wittgenstein's philosophy, both early and late, has been the radical question of meaning. His later work was a double shift. It moved from "how must I mean?" to "how do I in fact mean?" It also shifted the focus from the question of how I mean with my propositions to how my words mean. The conversion is to an a posteriori and empirical looking as well as to a deep respect for the role of use and usage. The early Wittgenstein had presumed that meaningful discourse requires an order in the world a priori and that the method of analysis could penetrate phenomena so as to reveal this universal structure as the standard for meaning and the source of certainty. He posited atoms of the world (simple objects) to parallel verbal atoms (names) in precise correspondence assured by a projective mental act (thinking). The later Wittgenstein saw that this whole metaphysical extrapolation had been blindly forced onto the ordinary and observable behavior of words. The impact of common usage had been ignored. An unnoticed grammar had erected a system.

> A simile that has been absorbed into the forms of our language produces a false appearance, and this disquiets us. "But this isn't how it is!" we say. "Yet this is how it has to be."⁶⁵

A picture forces itself upon us. We ignore our common sense about what is proper in our language because it seems it must be this way for us to mean at all. But, as we have seen, the turn to description breaks the tyranny of the picture of meaning. It also brings a healthy sense of the independence of language. Wittgenstein's new philosophy is a methodological shift in perspective which turns around the question of meaning.

The early Wittgenstein was an unwitting essentialist and a conscious atomist. But the later Wittgenstein discovered that words may mean in many different ways and that, in any case, simple objects and sharp conceptual boundaries are not necessarily available or sufficient to ground meaningfulness. There is no need to infer an exact calculus hooked into the world in mental projection. The claims of atomism and isomorphism were superfluous. A final analysis and a precise correlation prove to be illusory requirements for meaning.

Take, for example, a key feature of Wittgenstein's atomism. Description cannot confirm the analysis of facts into simple objects. Wittgenstein's insistence on a picturing structure included a special kind of object which survived all destruction and was absolutely simple. But when is an object too complex to be simple? How simple is simple? The simplicity of a "final analysis" is not a function of any metaphysical unit but of linguistic usage in a particular context.

> But what are the simple constituent parts of which reality is composed? What are the simple constituent parts of a chair?--The bits of wood of which it is made? Or the molecules, or the atoms?--"Simple" means not composite. And here

> the point is: in what sense "composite?" It makes
> no sense at all to speak absolutely of the "simple
> parts of a chair."[66]

The meaning of "complete analyis" is so vague that a theory of meaning relying on its possibility is useless. "Simple" and "composite" are relative terms. This is a startling, yet typically Wittgensteinian realization. To accept the root of the question as linguistic is to redirect the whole inquiry.[67] Placing the question in the new horizon of linguistic self-consciousness brings an end to the demand for simple objects, elementary propositions and the final analysis of a sentence. This is the typical Wittgensteinian procedure.

In summary, the <u>Philosophical Investigations</u> is an attempt to convert philosophers from two influential prejudices. (1) The first is the presumption that meaning is somehow the result of a correlation of words, thoughts and objects. From this perspective language is like cartography and when it is true it is very good cartography. This basic notion of representative isomorphism can generate an explanatory atomism or essentialism. These in turn may require positing sharp conceptual boundaries and imagining mysterious mental processes which fuse such concepts onto the world. At any rate, there is a tendency to seek and to find a special and permanent foundation for philosophical discourse. The search for such foundations is the major target of the later Wittgenstein's therapy. (2) A second philosophical prejudice accompanies the first: a chronic disregard for the role of what Wittgenstein calls "grammar." The compulsion to find security in ontology or epistemology leads the philosopher to overlook his less spectacular but more fundamental socio-linguistic roots. It is this myopia which allows the theory that meaning is a function of parallelism to stand and which exposes philosophy, unprotected, to shifting grammatical winds. There are no foundations in the usual philosophical sense of the word, but there is attention to language. (3) Conversion to a new horizon, to an empirically linguistic self-awareness, is the Wittgensteinian prescription for relief from these prejudices. The discovery of language-games is the occasion for his conversion. The corrective for grammatical oversight is careful attention to concrete cases. A good look at particular cases not only surfaces the grammar at work but also explodes the theory that all words mean in the same way. "A main cause of philosophical disease--a one-sided diet: one nourishes one's thinking with only one kind of example."[68] There is a disposition to abstract the "essence" of all of a word's uses and to ignore or refine away any use that contradicts that common element.[69] There is a tendency to find the sort of foundations one seeks. But it is possible to expand one's diet, to study paradigmatic examples and focus attention on particular differences. Attention to the games of language shatters the a priori picture of meaning which holds so many captive.

> You say: the point isn't the word, but its
> meaning, and you think of the meaning as a thing

of the same kind as the word, though also different from the word. Here the word, there the meaning. The money, and cow that you can buy with it. (But contrast: money, and its use.)[70]

(4) But if meaning is not something, it is not nothing either. The fact that meaning is not primarily a function of reference does not leave language completely untethered. The point of Wittgenstein's attack is to clear our heads and sharpen our attention. Asking what a word means puts us off in the wrong direction; one needs to ask instead how it is used. It is in the process of looking at actual use that the meaning appears. Further appeals to some object are therefore superfluous.[71] This appeal to use is not in any way an appeal to a new sort of object. Nothing could be less Wittgensteinian than making use into some esstential, sharply drawn and meaning-giving referent. The whole point of looking to use rather than to an object is not to fashion a new corresponding object but to rid ourselves of the constant and debilitating proclivity to assume that meaning must be more than a function of use in context. The destruction of this "cow and the money" template allows many philosophical knots to dissolve and brings the basic grammar of others into view.

This new appeal to use is not an appeal to any ontology or to language as a conceptual schema revealing that ontology. The requirement that meaning always have an ontological anchor is gratuitous: meaningfulness is located first by attending to grammar (use). This grammar may demand the company of a certain referent, but this need cannot be presumed and in any case is not the "foundational" factor. The origins of metaphysics itself are grammatical. There is no need to seek essences, parallel structures, or a coupling process. What is essential is to reject the picture of language as an ontologically derived cryptograph. For this reason the <u>Philosophical Investigations</u> strives to convert its readers not to yet another theory, but to a new horizon for viewing all theories. This conversion includes a turn away from the assumption that meaning is given by reference to objects. It fosters a propensity to beware of the confusion nurtured by the analogous grammars of various words. It allows us to develop the habit of looking at and learning from our use.

> When philosophers use a word—"knowledge," "being," object," "I," "proposition," "name,"—and try to grasp the <u>essence</u> of the thing, one must always ask oneself: is the word ever actually used in this way in the language-game which is its original home?
> What <u>we</u> do is to bring words back from their metaphysical to their everyday use.[72]

And so philosophy is become grammatical.

The later Wittgenstein is no longer interested in penetrating phenomena and discovering their essential structure. His inquiry is focused on the spatial and temporal phenomena of language, not on phantasms.[73] The rules or grammar of the language-game provide for meaning. The duties that philosophers would wish performed by essential correlations and extra-linguistic processes are actually the work of our grammar. "Essence is expressed by grammar."[74] Thus philosophical investigations begin by asking how a word is used and not by asking what item of experience always and only accompanies it. A typical Wittgensteinian move this: "One ought to ask, not what images are or what happens when one imagines anything, but how the word 'imagination' is used."[75] After all, "Grammar tells us what kind of object anything is."[76] And this grammar is a function of the larger culture.[77] Grammar is not just a single function, or a single use in a particular phrase, but the whole context; it is a matrix of objects, feelings, actions, gestures, etc., woven into the stream of life. Words mean by their context and use in the overall language-game or socio-linguistic life-setting. They are not rooted in some object or experience first but vice versa. Philosophical investigations, then, are conceptual; they are directed toward the linguistic context of philosophical problems, toward styles of life and language. The quest for transcendental, privileged foundations is abandoned for a sense of familiarity amid earthy, tangled streets of language.

But what does all this say to theologians? What sort of philosophical foundation does Wittgenstein offer to theology? Clearly he will not support any theology which appeals to a fundamental a priori order in the world or to a direct linking of words with a direct experience or direct knowledge. This would be to look in the wrong direction and to overlook what is most profound. Instead, Wittgenstein, as we have seen, suggests the value of a linguistic, empirical-observational, and methodological praxis. He insists on locating our final criteria in our actual language. This language is described by taking a good look at use. The ground is not language as we would like it but language as it is. The end point of all this is methodological in the most basic sense: it calls forth a shift in the performance. It generates a new horizon for doing philosophy. This horizon is characterized by the habitual suspicion that our difficulties may be conceptual and the concomitant tendency to recollect the concrete, ordinary context and usage of these concepts. The application of these facts to the situation becomes routine. "We want to replace wild conjectures and explanations by quiet weighing of linguistic facts."[78] This is a grounding in which metaphysical ravings and guesses are superceded by looking at language and taking it as it is. In the end this method offers a non-theoretical solution to the problem of foundations. Such a non-theoretical, non-foundational approach might be of use to theology in our empirical and pluralist culture. Foundational theology, then, would find its anchor not in a philosophy of language but in a linguistic method, which is to say, in a self-critical awareness of language. It would find its "foundations" in a shift away from concern with foundations.

Has theology made this linguistic turn? David Tracy's <u>Blessed Rage for Order</u> is a major work on doing theology and it places language at the center of its procedure. Undoubtedly it is some of the best fundamental theology available today. But has Tracy made language central to theology while at the same time embracing the sort of quest for foundations which Ludwig Wittgenstein found so impossible and wrong-headed? Does Tracy's search for foundations reflect the linguistic tropism with which Wittgenstein would infect us? In what sense are the foundations of David Tracy's theology linguistic?

Notes

1. Most of the recent works on Wittgenstein discuss the real continuity of his thought. One might refer to Kenny, <u>Wittgenstein</u>, pp. 219-32, Hallett, <u>Definition</u>, pp. 1-32, Hallett, <u>Companion</u>, pp. 23-57, or Peter Winch, "The Unity of Wittgenstein's Philosophy," in Peter Winch, ed., <u>Studies in the Philosophy of Wittgenstein</u> (London: Routledge & Kegan Paul, 1969). On the continuity of the theme of saying and showing in Wittgenstein's work see D. W. Harward, <u>Wittgenstein's Saying and Showing Themes</u> (Bonn: Bouvier, 1976) as well as the unpublished doctoral dissertation by Blanche L. Premo, <u>Wittgenstein's Notion of Description: From Logic to Grammar</u> (Marquette University, 1974). Wittgenstein's view of philosophy remained in basic continuity with T, 4.112, as quoted above in Chapter Three, note 64. The shift in his thought was a rejection only of its last paragraph and the attack on this position is a focal point of the <u>Investigations</u>: "Without philosophy thoughts are, as it were, cloudy and indistinct: its task is to make them clear and to give them sharp boundaries."

2. <u>PI</u>, 309.

3. <u>PI</u>, 132.

4. <u>PI</u>, 38.

5. <u>PI</u>, p. 216

6. The author of the <u>Tractatus</u> was concerned about essentialism (T, 3.323). The author of the <u>Investigations</u> saw this earlier route as unwittingly essentialist. While attacking the lack of reflection on language, the <u>Tractatus</u> had unreflectively presumed a universal and theoretical definition for terms such as "language" and "proposition." It is the concern of the later Wittgenstein to break the hold of this essentialism and to demolish as well the picture theory. Essentialism and the picture theory are separate errors. The early Wittgenstein was guilty of them both and the later Wittgenstein attempted to undermine them both.

7. It is important to note that this focus on misleading grammar is not an attempt to find a single prescribed use or meaning. Neither is it to suggest that there is only one cure for the philosopher's illnesses. This would be to put a universal and theoretical reading on what is essentially an ad hoc, non-theoretical practice. "When we say that by our method we try to counteract the misleading effect of certain analogies, it is important that you should understand that the idea of an analogy being misleading is nothing sharply defined." (<u>BB</u>, p. 28). For a survey of the various types of confusion pointed out by Wittgenstein under this rubric see Hallett, <u>Companion</u>, pp. 27-34.

8. PI, 66.

9. The following discussion especially reflects BB, pp. 17-19.

10. BB, p. 18. The history of philosophy is rife with examples. Plato's Meno comes to mind immediately.

11. BB, p. 18.

12. PI, 92.

13. PI, 90. Thus there is some merit to Finch calling Wittgenstein's later method "physiognomic phenomenalism" (Finch, pp. 169-91).

14. PI, 97.

15. PI, 97.

16. T, 3.3421: "And that is generally so in philosophy: again and again the individual case turns out to be unimportant, but the possibility of each individual case discloses something about the essence of the world." This summarizes a pivotal methodological issue between the later and the earlier Wittgenstein.

17. PI, 97.

18. PI, 96.

19. PI, 255.

20. PI, 309.

21. PI, 101. Wittgenstein's own essentialism took the form of a logical atomism. He was dazzled by the so-called ideal order. "The ideal, as we think of it, is unshakable. You can never get outside it; you must always turn back. There is no outside; outside you cannot breathe. Where does this idea come from? It is like a pair of glasses on our nose through which we see whatever we look at. It never occurs to us to take them off." (PI, 103).

22. PI, 107. Wittgenstein elaborates later: 'But this is how it is-------' I say to myself over and over again. I feel as though, if only I could fix my gaze absolutely sharply on this fact, get it in focus, I must grasp the essence of the matter." (PI, 113). "(Tractatus Logico-Philosophicus, 4.5): 'The general form of propositions is: this is how things are.' That is the kind of proposition that one repeats to oneself countless times. One thinks that one is tracing the outline of the thing's nature over and over again, and one is merely tracing round the frame through which we look at." PI, 114.

23. <u>PI</u>, 123.

24. <u>PI</u>, p. ix.

25. <u>PI</u>, 18.

26. <u>PI</u>, 115.

27. <u>BB</u>, p. 6.

28. <u>PI</u>, 126.

29. <u>PI</u>, 122.

30. <u>PI</u>, p. ix: "The thoughts which I publish in what follows are the precipitate of philosophical investigations which have occupied me for the last sixteen years. They concern many subjects: the concepts of meaning, of understanding, of a proposition, of logic, the foundations of mathematics, states of consciousness, and other things. I have written down all these thoughts as <u>remarks</u>, short paragraphs, of which there is sometimes a fairly long chain about the same subject, while I sometimes make a sudden change, jumping from one topic to another."

31. "This brings us to the question of what his separate <u>Bermerkungen</u> are. A great many of them are separate in the sense that one could read each of them without looking before or after; and someone who heard that the author made two quite different arrangements of a lot of the same material might guess that they were all like that. But that is far from being the case. There is very often a necessary connection between one remark and its predecessor, say in the form of a demonstrative whose reference is, or is given in, the predecessor. Whatever the arrangement of the material as a whole, such connections were preserved. So that the building blocks for the different structures are <u>not</u> quite generally the separate <u>Bermerkungen</u>, but may be these or may be short runs of them." G. E. M. Anscombe, "On the Form of Wittgenstein's Writing," in Raymond Klibansky, ed., <u>Contemporary Philosophy: A Survey</u>, III (Florence: Italia Editrice, 1969), p. 376. It is possible to prepare a thematic outline of the <u>Investigations</u>. See, for example, Judith Genova, "A Map of the <u>Philosophical Investigations</u>," <u>Philosophical Investigations</u> 1 (Winter 1978): 41-56.

32. <u>PI</u>, 43.

33. <u>PI</u>, 7. So a certain explanation of meaning only makes sense if one can play the game within which it is sensible. For example, one cannot explain the king in a game of chess by saying "this piece is the king," if the pupil has never played chess, or does not know a game with pieces, or has never watched others play a game and understood how they were going on. Only if someone knows games can you explain what a game-piece is and only if he knows what a game-piece is can you tell him

111

how a particular piece moves. "This piece is the king" will tell him the use of the piece only if the stage has already been set for such an explanation. So it is with words: their meaning comes from their role in a particular language-game. See PI, 31. "We may say: <u>nothing</u> has so far been done, when a thing has been named. It has not even <u>got</u> a name except in the language-game." PI, 49.

34. Z, 173.

35. PI, 340.

36. PI, 5.

37. BB, p. 17. The role of the language-game is summed up in PI, 130: "Our clear and simple language-games are not preparatory studies for a future regularization of language—as it were first approximations, ignoring friction and air-resistance. The language-games are rather set up as <u>objects of comparison</u> which are meant to throw light on the facts of our language by way not only of similarities, but also of dissimilarities."

38. One sees this method at work from the beginning of the Philosophical Investigations. Recall that Wittgenstein begins with a quotation from St. Augustine which he feels summarizes a view of meaning to be attacked. He follows this with a succinct description of a similar theory propunded by his own Tractatus Logico-Philosophicus. The next move is to raise some doubts about this view of meaning by mentioning the homey example of sending someone to the grocery with a slip of paper marked "five red apples." He wonders how the shopkeeper knows what to do and notes that all three words in this note move with different uses. These remarks comprise the first number of the Investigations. Wittgenstein brings this theory to full stature in number two. There he imagines a language for which the "Augustinian" account would be true: "Let us imagine a language for which the description given by Augustine is right. The language is meant to serve for communication between a builder A and an assistant B. A is building with buildingstone; there are blocks, pillars, slabs and beams. B has to pass the stones, and that in the order in which A needs them. For this purpose they use a language consisting of the words "block," "pillar," "slab," "beam." A calls them out;—B brings the stone which he has learnt to bring at such-and-such a call.----Conceive this as a complete primitive language." This use of the simple "slab" language is what he calls, in PI 48, "the method of number two." It is followed by remarks which highlight its confusion and also develop the notion of the language-game. A tone for the remaining investigations is set. Taking a theory seriously and looking at it through an accurate concrete example makes clear the way in which language is working in that theory. This is a method for the imaginative observation of language at work.

39. PI, 127.

40. PI, 120.

41. PI, 11, 14.

42. PI, 12.

43. BB, p. 1.

44. PI, 66.

45. PI, 67.

46. BB, pp. 1-2. The example is primarily an attack on Schlick's version of ostensive definition, viz., that ostensive definition alone--with no help from language--is the source of meaning.

47. PI, 30, 31, 49.

48. PI, p. 190. For a helpful, if overly systematic, discussion of Wittgenstein's use of the term "grammar," see Ernst Konrad Specht, The Foundations of Wittgenstein's Late Philosophy, trans. D. E. Walford (New York: Barnes & Noble, 1969), pp. 144-52.

49. Z, 395.

50. Z, 173.

51. Z, 532, 534.

52. LC, p. 2.

53. PI, p. 224.

54. BB, p. 7. See also BB, p. 26.

55. Z, 458.

56. The example of these three statements is suggested and discussed in K. T. Fann, Witgenstein's Conception of Philosophy (Berkley: University of California Press, 1971), pp. 89-93.

57. BB, p. 23.

58. "It is part of the grammar of the word 'chair' that this is what we call 'to sit on a chair,' and it is part of the grammar of the word 'meaning' that this is what we call 'explanation of meaning,' in the same way to explain my criterion for another person's having toothache is to give a grammatical explanation about the word 'toothache.'" (BB, p. 24). Failure to look to grammar leads to chronic philosophical misdirection: "Here it is easy to get into that dead end in philosophy, where one

believes that the difficulty of the task consists in our having to describe phenomena that are hard to get a hold of, the present experience that slips quickly by, or something of the kind. Where we find ordinary language too crude, and it looks as if we were having to do, not with the phenomena of every day, but with ones that 'easily elude us, and, in their coming to be and passing away, produce those others an average effect.'" (PI, 436).

59. Z, 459.

60. Z, 55.

61. BB, p. 27.

62. To say that our philosophical foundations are linguistic is not to trivialize the problems of philosophy but to admit their profundity. "The problems arising through a misinterpretation of our forms of language have the character of depth. They are deep disquietudes; their roots are as deep in us as the forms of our language and their significance is as great as the importance of our language." PI, 111.

63. PI, 109.

64. PI, 645.

65. PI, 112.

66. PI, 47. Later in this same number Wittgenstein says, "Asking 'is this object composite?' outside a particular language-game is like what a boy once did, who had to say whether the verbs in certain sentences were in the active or passive voice, and who racked his brains over the question whether the verb 'to sleep' meant something active or passive."

67. "To the philosophical question 'Is the visual image of this tree composite, and what are its component parts?' the correct answer is: 'That depends on what you understand by "composite".' (And that is of course not an answer but a rejection of the question.)" PI, 47.

68. PI, 589.

69. See the discussion in BB, pp. 17-20, especially the following remarks from pp. 19-20: "The idea that in order to get clear about the meaning of a general term one had to find the common element in all its applications has shackled philosophical investigation; for it has not only led to no result, but also made the philosopher dismiss as irrelevant the concrete cases, which alone could have helped him to understand the usage of the general term. When Socrates asks the question 'what is knowledge?' he does not even regard it as a preliminary answer to enumerate cases of knowledge."

70. PI, 120.

71. O. K. Bouwsma reviews the issue nicely in "The Blue Book," as reprinted in Fann, Ludwig Wittgenstein, pp. 165-69.

72. PI, 116. "When we do philosophy we are like savages, primitive people, who hear the expressions of civilized men, put a false interpretation on them, and then draw the queerest conclusions from it." PI, 194.

73. PI, 108.

74. PI, 371.

75. PI, 370. This paradigm is explained in the rest of the number: "But that does not mean that I want to talk only about words. For the question as to the nature of the imagination is as much about the word 'imagination' as my question is. And I am only saying that this question is not to be decided—neither for the person who does the imagining, nor for anyone else—by pointing; nor yet by a description of any process. The first question also asks for a word explained; but it makes us expect a wrong kind of answer."

76. PI, 373. This statement is the context for the famous parenthesis which follow it: "(Theology as grammar.)" See also Z, 144: "How words are understood is not told by words alone. (Theology)."

77. LC, 5; PI, 206; PI, p. 174.

78. Z, 447. The earlier part of this number provides an interesting remark on this shift in methodological horizon: "Disquiet in philosophy might be said to arise from looking at philosophy wrongly, seeing it wrong, namely as if it were divided into (infinite) longitudinal stripes instead of into (finite) cross strips. This inversion in our conception produces the greatest difficulty. So we try as it were to grasp the unlimited strips and complain that it cannot be done piecemeal. To be sure it cannot, if by a piece one means an infinite longitudinal strip. But it may well be done, if one means a cross-strip.—But in that case we never get to the end of our work!—Of course not, for it has no end."

CHAPTER FIVE
BEGINNING AT THE BEGINNING:
WITTGENSTEIN AND FOUNDATIONAL THEOLOGY

David Tracy's revisionism expresses a fundamental commitment to the open and public nature of theological inquiry. He is convinced of the necessity of remaining faithful to the religious tradition of Christianity and to the intellectual tradition of a scientific community of inquirers. Any worthwhile theology will share this same commitment. Methodological self-consciousness is the key to this religious and intellectual credibility. It is a source of security in a secular and pluralistic world. For Tracy, this search for foundations is finally a search for criteria of meaning and truth in theological discourse. The quest for a public, methodological and empirical theology generates a fundamental focus on language. But one may ask, especially from a Wittgensteinian perspective, whether Tracy has properly filled his own prescription. Has he brought theological inquiry to a more useful and more solid footing? Does revisionism begin at the beginning? Wittgenstein was no theologian. But he did understand the search for foundations and the need for clarity in inquiry. Wittgenstein knew from experience that it was possible to build on linguistic foundations and yet overlook language. "It is difficult to begin at the beginning. And not try to go further back."[1]

This remark of Wittgenstein's is both a confession and a warning. David Tracy does try to try to go further back. Both Tracy and Wittgenstein see the usefulness of looking to language for help with philosophical and foundational puzzels. But this general sympathy is not at all agreement. Tracy and Wittgenstein take radically different views of method and language. David Tracy is involved in a search for foundations, a quest for epistemological and metaphysical guarantees in doing theology. Ludwig Wittgenstein, though once a victim of similar desires, has rejected the quest for such foundations as misdirected. Tracy wants to explain what we can say by reference to the authority of phenomenology and metaphysics. Wittgenstein is convinced that what society lets us say is the authority for phenomenology and metaphysics. This is not a clash of theories, but of perspectives.

David Tracy is convinced that the source and core of both religious symbol and philosophical thought is pre-reflective and even pre-linguistic. The success of various reflective controls of meaning includes the ability to reflect critically upon our root experience of existence (hermeneutics of suspicion), but is essentially a function of their ability to simply reflect this experience in more differentiated contexts (hermeneutics of recollection).[2] The epistemology behind Tracy's revisionism is indebted to a Ricoeurian conviction that "symbol gives rise to thought." The intellectual disciplines of philosophy and theology deal with the conscious thematization (the belief level) of an essentially pre-reflective experience (the faith level). The standard for the correct analysis of beliefs is always fidelity to the basic experience which originated them. For Tracy this hermeneutic epistemology is to be supplemented with an analysis of this grounding experience patterned on Ogden's presentation of our most basic experience: the pre-linguistic origins of religion and philosophy are found in the non-sensuous experience of the self as a self which yields a basic trust and sense of unity with something greater.[3] The methodological search for criteria of meaning and truth applicable to theology ends in the disclosure of the pre-reflective ground of our pre-linguistic faith experience. Tracy's path to a fundamental theology is the achievement of a sort of second naivete. It is a critical going home, a conscious, intellectually differentiated appropriation of the faith behind beliefs. It provides a method which is nothing if not an appeal to experience.

The project Tracy envisions--concrete working out of a "philosophical reflection upon the meanings present" in common human experience and the Christian fact[4]--is a fundamental theology which discloses its own experiential adequacy. The criteria which guide his method turn out to be a function of the source he posits for these "meanings," viz., our experience of self including basic faith experience and an intimation of our union with a whole. By tapping into this experience Tracy establishes a referent for "religious" and so guarantees its meaningfulness. By tapping into this experience he establishes the accuracy of the theistic conception of this experience and therefore guarantees its truth. It is always some aspect of basic faith which makes the terms "religious" and "God" meaningful and true.

The major theses which set the operation of Tracy's foundational theology concern (1) the nature and scope of the basic faith experience and (2) the link between this experience and its expressions, especially language. No matter how differently Tracy defines experience, it remains that experience is the foundation of his theology, the ultimate clue that one is proceeding aright. Tracy's approach is linguistic to the extent that it takes as one of its immediate concerns language; language is an important entree to our root experience. But he is concerned not with use and usage but with a referent that must supply meaningfulness and truth. Talk of religion and God is intellectually acceptable if a public referent in experience can be located. Tracy's task is to show the link between experience and its expression. The examination of meaning and truth becomes an examination of the vehicles for the expression of our basic experience. Language is not the source of meaning, but reflects the meaningfulness given by experience. It is experience, not language, which is the focal point of Tracy's method and the facilitator of public discourse.

Wittgenstein too was interested in the foundations for philosophical inquiry. Or better, Wittgenstein was interested in disabusing philosophers of their fixation on finding "foundations." His journeyings are a paradigm of philosophical disorientation and of the cure effected by getting a synoptic view of our linguistic landscape. The early Wittgenstein, like so many philosophers, had resisted a full linguistic turn. Language was important but, in a sense, not fundamental. For all of the talk about language, the final criteria for meaning and truth emerged not in language itself but in the ability of language to mirror the world. This mirror later proved to be an illusion. Wittgenstein discovered that the way out of philosophical puzzles is at once more obvious and more subtle.

The search for foundations is often an essentialist venture. It becomes a tautologous investigation, a function of overt and covert definition a priori. It is often a quest for the structure of meaning. It presumes an alignment of language, thought and the world which must be the key to meaning. The final standard is ontological and referential. For the mature Wittgenstein, essence is expressed by grammar and meaning tends to be given by use. Family resemblance appears where sharply bordered concepts should have been, a priori correlation evaporates in the face of a posteriori use, and description proves more revealing than analysis. There are no foundations. The bedrock of philosophy is not ontological but socio-linguistic. Final justification lies first in language and not in language as a representation of something else.

Philosophers do not need a special and compelling ground for their knowledge. It will not bring them relief and clarity. What is helpful is attention to language. But this is not really a "foundation" in the usual sense. It is a therapeutic and methodological imperative. The Wittgensteinian shift is a turn to language and away from foundations. It is not a new linguistic foundation. Philosophy has not been transformed into philology or linguistics nor has it surrendered to the theoretical pictures offered by other disciplines. Philosophical investigations look to the ordinary use and boundaries of our ordinary language. In so doing they hope to cure the chronic overlooking of language which fosters radically incomplete and confused philosophical thinking. If one made these ordinary linguistic facts into philosophical theses "it would never be possible to debate them because everyone would agree to them."[5] Of course language is important. Theoretical formulations of the obvious are not helpful. But a practical and personal assembling of reminders may trigger a profound and practical conversion. A thesis is not a praxis. The problem is not theoretical but practical. The desire for philosophical foundations must be abandoned. Radical inattention to language is cured by a radical shift in methodological disposition. "The real discovery is the one that makes me capable of stopping doing philosophy when I want to."[6] Can there be a foundation for this? What foundation is at work when a fly is freed from a fly-bottle?

David Tracy insists on an epistemological and metaphysical foundation for theological inquiry. This fixation on the determinative role of experience brings with it a tendency to overlook the fundamental import of our ordinary language. Language is seen as important in perceiving and liberating the real criterion for public theology--experience. This view contains a striking presumption about how language must mean. This presumption about the re-presentative nature of language suggests to Tracy the practical value of a hermeneutic phenomenology and a neo-classical metaphysic. Their function is to disclose foundational experiences. To set the criteria for theology is to encapsulate in an intellectual pattern the experiential foundations of religious discourse. Foundational theology is a religiously sensitive form of philosophical inquiry. And philosophical investigations, for Tracy, are factual investigations.

There is a need for clarity in theological investigations. This is precisely why David Tracy insists on getting clear about criteria for meaningfulness and truth. He sees the justification of theology as the revelation of a referent, the disclosure of a public, shared experience. This basic faith experience can be surfaced in each of theology's two sources, correlated, and metaphysically validated. The term "religious" may be given a limited denotation. Theology is advised to proceed by the phenomenological description and metaphysical validation of experience and its language.

> Both disciplines must be involved in "philosophical reflection upon our common human experience and language" in a manner that might be said to include two movements: a phenomenological moment to disclose the meaning and meaningfulness of that experience and a transcendental moment to disclose the true conditions of the possibility of that experience.[7]

"Meaning" is a matter of internal coherence and consistent use. A concept is considered "meaningful" if it mediates the immediate experience of the self-as-a-self. "Truth" is a matter of the ground and necessity of this primordial experience itself.[8] There is a whole world of definition and assumption in this summary statement of the revisionist project. Phenomenology and metaphysics habitually look <u>to</u> experience and only <u>through</u> language. A certain confusion may result from this oversight.

Attention to use is important for fruitful inquiry. One does tend to think too much about meaning and not look enough. This inattention may then begin to direct one's inquiry. Unnoticed conceptual moves may seem to be factual disclosures. Definitions may appear to be empirical discoveries and assertions. The waters here are deep and treacherous. Failure to grasp clearly the function of a concept (e.g., "truth" or "meaningfulness") begets factual-sounding questions (e.g., "What is meaningfulness?") which subtly redirect the inquiry. Such a misstep does trouble <u>Blessed Rage for Order</u>. There is a certain lack of clarity surrounding some of the very concepts which Tracy would like to sharpen. This cloudiness is related to the unchallenged presumption that meaningful language must be re-presentational.

Words and Confusion

There is a certain conceptual looseness in Tracy's work. As he discusses "limits-to" and "grounds-of" one feels as if one knows what

Tracy means and yet does not quite know. Tracy wants to fix these concepts firmly, but they resist and tend to remain elastic. We do understand the usage of the word "limit," for example, but its use in Blessed Rage for Order is not ordinary. What exactly could not count as limit language and experience? Are peak experiences always in fact limit experiences? Why is that? There is more than appeal to bald experience here. There is reliance on a special definition of ordinary terms. Such terms as "ultimate," "worthwhile," and "final" are notoriously ambiguous in philosophical argument. Often they provide cover for the premature importation of conclusions. This is the very kind of uncritical subjectivity which Tracy wishes to prevent. He wants more than tautologous meaning. But his antidote is to talk at length about experience. He proceeds as if some sort of pointing would make the meaning of these concepts absolutely clear. Such an overlooking of a word's linguistic baggage is hazardous. The simple discussion of various experiences is not sufficient to convey the meaning of a concept, for there is also the whole matter of use in a context.

Is "ultimate" a description or a definition? Words like "ultimate" or "worthwhile" sometimes function as seals of approval rather than as serious empirical descriptions. They reveal what an author finds satisfying rather than what is obvious to the casual observer. They constitute a judgment about where and when an inquiry may rest. It is important to recall that "ultimate" is not an absolute term but a judgment that further digging may be fruitless. Are "limits-to" borders drawn, or simply described? One is free to draw boundaries and to set conceptual borders. But not remarking on this fact does set an investigation adrift with a faulty compass. It may lead the explorer to think he is proceeding in the direction of factual exploration and charting factual "limits," when his investigations are conceptual and his limits grammatical.

How does Tracy know that a particular experience is our "basic" faith? How basic is this "most basic" confidence? Tracy proceeds by pointing out particular experiences and claiming that these are logically and empirically fundamental. But how obvious is this, even when it is pointed out? One man's ultimacy may be another man's superficiality. Perhaps the ultimate experience of the human is fear of death and a suspicion that human living is an insignificant and absurd lie. Such convictions are hardly novel, yet this is not Tracy's description of our basic faith. Which description is correct? Which experience is "really" ultimate and which is merely a symptom? A leper might consult a priest, a psychologist, and a dermatologist. Which one is treating the <u>ultimate</u> source of her sickness? The confusion is generated by the positing of free-floating terms, terms advanced as clear on their own and irrespective of any particular context. What is needed for clarity is not a closer look at the experience but a closer look at the use of the concept.

> To the <u>philosophical</u> question: "Is the visual image of this tree composite, and what are its component parts?" the correct answer is: "That depends on

what you understand by 'composite'." (And that is, of course, not an answer but a rejection of the question.)[9]

Philosophical investigations require conceptual attentiveness. Ultimacy and superficiality (and complexity) are a function of the context of general usage and particular use. Saying "But these particulars and experiences do exist" does not establish the meaning of the words "ultimate" or "composite." What does happen, of course, is that a context is unconsciously projected and a workable meaning thereby selected.[10]

There are other instances where the distinction between definition and observation seems cloudy. The key notion in David Tracy's solution to the problems of fundamental theology is basic faith, its commonality and its truly religious nature. He claims that it is our "...fundamental faith in the ultimate worth of our life here and now which constitutes the basic faith common to the committed secular thinker and the committed Christian alike...."[11] This is the linchpin of revisionism.

> An explicit and full recognition of this faith as, in fact, the common faith shared by secularist and modern Christians is perhaps the most important insight needed to understand the contemporary theological situation in its full dimensions and its real possibilities.[12]

But how is this faith established as "common?" How is it established as "secular?" As "religious?" Tracy hopes that affirming various experiences will establish them as both secular and religious.

The interplay of the words "implicit" and "explicit" in Tracy's discussion sets the possibility of a common faith. The simple application of these terms accomplishes much. There is no discussion of use. The terms are justified by appeal to the experience at hand. It is the "same" (another troublesome word in philosophy) experience dressed differently in different contexts. Explicitly religious language and experience are implicitly secular, explicitly secular language and experience are implicitly religious. A common ground between two commonly separated realms is established in the movement from explicit to implicit as allowed by reference to an experience. "Explicit" is used to indicate the usual, common, and unsurprising uses of the term "religious." "Implicit" is used to designate Tracy's new and wider use of the term. The assertion is that the secular and the religious are—despite differences of vocabulary and ordinary use—on one level and by one definition, identical. But this ontological and existential fact of commonality may be to a great extent a grammatical achievement.

Is this basic faith "the common faith" of secularist and religious alike? Do all secularists have this confidence in the worth of their lives? Is such a basic faith "presupposed by all our existing and understanding?"[13] This is the faith of pessimists, suicides and nihilists? What can this mean? Someone like Ernst Becker might claim that human experience is at root an experience of terror. Culture, art, and religion are frantic denials of our death. They are attempts to compensate for the overwhelmingly negative and fearful experience of being human.[14] Can this analysis be reinterpreted into a basic confidence? Can it be excised as not truly secular? Are the borders of the concept to be redrawn so as to exclude Sartre, Camus, Becker, and many others? What is to be gained by invoking an extraordinary sense of "secular" which denies their mind? A theory that works. But what does one accomplish? Disguising value judgments and definitions as compelling empirical observations does not advance theological inquiry.

The confusion is the result of jumping back and forth between the definition of concepts and the pointing to experiences, while ignoring the role the former plays in the latter. "Here the temptation to believe in a phenomenology, something midway between science and logic, is very great."[15] Tracy's assertions about "secular man" are not scientific or statistical or logical but phenomenological. In this way he hopes to retain the appeal to experience but to avoid the naive positing of an already-out-there-now-real. He does not want to factor out the concrete human person. Still, phenomenology sets the problematic as a radical attention to the structures of experience and this selective focus blurs the linguistic environment. After all, experience is described, understood and judged in language. Failure to note the performance of the linguistic variable may skew one's inquiry. While attention is directed to experience, a definition of "secular man" is quietly at work.

One is uneasy with Tracy's discussion. He attempts to fix the borders of concepts once and for all. But ordinary usage continues, willy-nilly, to suggest other uses and to display the linguistic confusion. Van Harvey senses this very difficulty when he remarks on the odd use of the word "confidence" in Blessed Rage for Order:

> If the meaning of "confidence" is so revised that it is made synonymous with living itself and, hence, never can be lost so long as we are alive, then we will be forced to coin some other synonym for confidence that denotes that attitude which we use in contrast to "fear," "terror," and "anxiety" within life.[16]

The ordinary sense is being altered. If it is not altered, the thesis becomes false. In his discussion of secular experience, Tracy is asserting a new use, but, failing to see the move as linguistic, presumes to be noting the revelation of our secular faith. Such special definition is not argument. It may not even be useful and certainly may be confusing. What is the "cash value" of a concept so broad that no one can be excluded or so narrow that nothing new or interesting can be included? The confusion of the factual and the grammatical is not the way to clarity. To ask what is meant by claiming something as the common faith or as under all existing and understanding is not mere nit-picking. It is a way to attend to language. It is a way to attend to philosophical and theological problems. The clarity derived soley from definition of terms may be genuine, but it is the banal, uninteresting clarity of truism and tautology. This is the result of a craving for generality in theology, of the tendency to propose theories and to adjust terms so that those theories cannot be found in error. "If one tried to advance theses in philosophy, it would never be possible to debate them, because everyone would agree with them."[17]

Similar problems trouble Tracy's account of "religious" and "religion." His use of these terms is peculiar and limited. "This moment, if authentically religious, will be experienced as a limit-experience and will be expressed in a limit-language representative of that insight and that experience."[18] There is something unsettled here. Can the term "religious" be reserved only for the re-presentation of basic faith? Are all limit experiences and expressions necessarily instances of the religious? Why? What would count as a counter-example? For many people, the fact of human suffering is a denial of religion. For some humans, peak experiences are regularly associated with a sadomasochistic ritual. One may claim that the experience of the void and the experience of basic confidence are one. It does seem confusing. There is a rerouting of ordinary use. Are these limit-experiences religious? Furthermore, are not these experiences facts of biology, anthropology and psychology? Why insist that they are also religious? It is unclear. Our confusion is conceptual, yet Tracy does not reflect enough on his use of language. Instead he looks to experience for clarity.

Tracy's argument does get somewhere, but it is moved by the unnoticed power of his own use of words. What sort of definition of religion encompasses everyone, even those who disavow any experience of basic confidence and are wary of anything religious? With so great an extension, does this definition have any comprehension? Religion is defined in terms designed to avoid the supernatural elements and to stress natural, secular elements. There is a craving for generality which dismisses recalcitrant particulars. Once religion is defined in terms of a common and secular essence, it is not difficult to reveal the essentially religious nature of the secular.

> On one level, one may recall that religious language is basically re-presentative as making present anew, through symbolic expression, a human reality (for example, our basic trust in the worthwhileness of existence). . . .[19]

But why not then drop the term "religious" and simply speak of the secular? Would the religious person agree that his religion is the re-presentation of "a human reality" and "none other than the most adequate articulation of the basic faith of secularity itself?"[20] Would the secularist want to affirm this as anonymous religiosity? Or would both sense a certain sleight of hand in the argument? It may be possible to redefine "religious" in this sort of phenomenological move, but then we need some other word to use in distinguishing the non-religious from the religious. Or do we? A confusion enters the debate when one presumes a scientific exactness for ordinary words.[21] One wonders if a ground not formerly noted is being revealed or if matters have merely gotten more verbally complex. How useful is a definition of religion that excludes no one? Very useful, if your theory is that religion must include everyone. Tracy points out certain experiences and expects that only they can be experientially linked to all uses of "religious." The borders of a concept are being sharpened to allow for more precise discussing and disclosure. But a price is paid here for this willful precision: Is the discussion factually informative?

As presented in <u>Blessed Rage for Order</u>, religion must be re-presentative, it must come to expression in limit-language, it must express limit-experience, and these in turn must reveal our basic experience of self. According to whom? Is this a scientific statement? A logical statement? What is going on here? Is "religion" ordinarily used in this way? Are we not at first puzzled to hear that the religious and the non-religious are both religious--in a sense? Is this assertion allowed by new data or by new definitions?

> When philosophers use a word--"knowledge," "being," "object," "I," "proposition," "name"--and try to grasp the <u>essence</u> of the thing, one must always ask oneself: is the word ever actually used in this way in the language-game which is its original home?[22]

The word "religious" is taking on a new life. It is being detached from its natural history, fixed, and isolated in one particular use. Tracy's claims about religion and the religious are the result of a fascination with theory making. They are symptomatic of the philosophical and theological tendency to ignore particulars in favor of a common essence, and to presume that a word will present the identical performance in any and all contexts.

Does Tracy's theory about religion and re-presentation apply to all uses of "religion" and "religious" and only to these? There are fuzzy areas. When is faith "ultimate?" When is an experience properly tagged "limit?" When not? Does every human in fact have basic faith as described by David Tracy? Is this what religion in fact is? When language is thematizing the experience of limit and self, what is gained by bringing in talk about "religion" and "God?" Does one need these concepts to note limits or to affirm that life is worthwhile? What additional mechanism does the additional word "religious" move? If the word "religious" is being used in the ordinary way, there leap to mind several concrete examples which deny the theory that all religion is re-presentative of a common trust. If these misgivings do not invalidate the theory, then there must be some odd sense of the various terms at work. As Tracy begins to explain away this oddity, the argument becomes clearer and the terms become more limited. They are withdrawn from the weave of life and frozen at one point in one context. This may cause problems in using a term in public discourse. The terms of a theory are often adjusted so as to exclude contrary data and "tighten" the theory. But there is always danger that such a maneuver will present a theory that is not factually informative or interesting. One's theory may be reduced to putting forth truism (e.g., religion can feel good) or tautology (e.g., religion is re-presentative because basic faith is presented and thematized in all occurrences of the religious). The point is that letting "religious" wander about unattended is not fruitful. Keeping it on an artificial tether can be confusing. The factual and the conceptual may get confused. The more unnoticed our language is, the less light is likely to be shed on the problem under consideration. One gets involved in the dubious project of classifying clouds by their shapes. "What we do is to bring words back from their metaphysical to their everyday use."[23]

  We ask about ordinary use not in order to rule out special use, but to highlight such uses as special and thereby to signal a dangerous intersection for the philosophical inquirer. Tracy wants to operate a clear and public investigation. He wants his words to be exact and coherent. This is what he calls "meaning." In his view "meaning" (conceptual borders) is a direct result of disclosing appropriate experiences. It requires "a phenomenological moment to disclose the meaning. . . ."[24] This leads to a radical disregard for language, except as a carrier for experience. And this oversight brings just what it seeks to avoid: uncertainty about meaning. The meaning of several important terms seems rather unsettled. It is not clear that Tracy's use is in line with the usual use of the word. It is not clear that it is not. It is not clear why (or if) these words suddenly mean this and only this. There is room for confusion. Tracy himself occasionally uses the term "meaning" not in his special sense of coherence, but to indicate what he usually prefers to call "meaningfulness."[25] The greatest danger in forgetting that one has proposed a special use of an ordinary term, is that he may not be careful to mark this linguistic advance off from his empirical assertions. Scientific investigations are factual investigations, philosophical investigations are conceptual investigations, and confusing the two is notoriously counter-productive.

  Tracy wants his words to have "meaning" absolutely, whatever their particular context and common usage. But words have meaning only in the stream of life, in the flow of usage, in a particular context. Words have meaning in a matrix of particulars. To remove them from this stream is to risk at least confusion and at most the formulation of a hollow argument. For Tracy meaning is guaranteed by lining up particular experiences. What he calls "meaningfulness" is also proven in that way. Tracy's vision is too narrow. Experience may be part of the meaning of a particular word, but words do not wear their interpretation on their sleeves.

Experience does not speak for itself, it does not carry a name badge. "We may say: <u>nothing</u> has so far been done, when a thing has been named. It has not even <u>got</u> a name except in the language-game."[26]

A Captivating Picture

David Tracy's foundational theology is controlled by and derived from his presumption that language, especially "religious language," is re-presentative. This picture is reflected in the major moves and methods of his revisionism. It allows Tracy to construct a project which is centered on the revelation of experience and the connection of these disclosures with appropriately religious and secular language. Talk of re-presentation turns attention to what is re-presented and how well. It shapes Tracy's statement of how theology can be public, revisionist, empirical, linguistic, and methodological. The starting point for Tracy's revisionism is the possibility of a critical correlation of our common human experience and the Christian fact. It is the representational nature of language which allows Tracy to strike a revisionist attitude toward these sources. Correlation is possible because each source is fundamentally re-presentative. Furthermore, revision and mutual critique are a fact because each source re-presents the same secular-religious experience. Phenomenology is the primary method of investigation precisely because it presumes the same representational schema of meaning and claims to liberate the required experiences. The metaphysics selected functions on a similar presupposition. But does this approach bring clarity to theological investigations? Does it get Tracy where he wants to go? The assertion that religious language is disclosive language is an essential in the revisionist construction of a public theology. The focus is sqarely on experience. Finding and relating a common experience is the crucial move. Tracy does not look at his language to see if it is re-presentative, or how it might be. Rather, he presumes a priori that it must be and then seeks the requisite experiences. In the process, a whole isomorphic template for meaning is smuggled in and positioned in such a way that it appears to have been there from the beginning. Questions of meaningfulness and truth for Tracy are not questions about the uses of language, but about the reality which language mirrors. And so again, the overlooking of language begins a confusion.

The journey down the road to foundationalism and linguistic oversight begins in Tracy's definition of his project. Theological reflection is to begin with analysis of common human experience and language as well as explicitly religious experience and language. The project is to be a reflection on "meanings."

> More exactly, the revisionist model for Christian theology ordinarily bears some such formulation as the following: contemporary Christian theology is best understood as philosophical reflection upon the meanings present in common human experience and the meanings present in the Christian tradition.[27]

Meanings are the focus of foundational theological inquiry. They are the subject of investigation, the objects of correlation, and the point of departure for metaphysical validation. Tracy calls for a theology that is "appropriate to the central meanings of the secular faith we share and to the central meanings represented in the Christian tradition."[28] Why all this talk in <u>Blessed Rage for Order</u> about the presence, disclosure and location of "meanings?" As Tracy sees it, his critics claim that our language about religion is unintelligible because it has no referent. He takes it as his task to find such a referent and to locate it in the public domain. Accepting the problematic as set by such critics is a serious misstep. For Tracy, meanings turn out to be self-understandings which arise from our basic experience of self. But however they are construed—as objects, feelings, halos, etc.—Tracy's discussion of "meanings" sets him off in the wrong direction. It helps him to ontologize the question of meaningfulness and so to overlook use.

To speak of "meanings" turns one's head in the direction of substantives. This move fosters the assumption that language must be re-presentative. Tracy uses the nouns "meaning" and "meaningfulness" extensively. His use subtly suggest quasi-objects. Meaningfulness is the presence of meanings. To be meaningful is to have meanings. Willy-nilly one begins to think of meanings as something like isolable entities, the atoms of our common human experience and Christian symbols, which make theological discourse work. A perspective is forming.

> The questions "What is length?," "What is meaning?," "What is the number one?" etc., produce in us a mental cramp. We feel that we can't point to anything in reply to them and yet ought to point to something. (We are up against one of the great sources of philosophical bewilderment: a substantive makes us look for a thing that corresponds to it.)[29]

A factual-sounding inquiry may lead us into grammatical confusion. Thinking of the question of meaningfulness as a question about the "what" sets us off on a bad footing. The familiar pattern of name-object thinking is quietly setting up shop. Has Tracy found the proper referent? Occupied with the problem of whether Tracy's answer is correct, one may fail to notice the misleading heuristic of his question.

> The question itself keeps the mind pressing against a blank wall, thereby preventing it from ever finding the outlet. To show a man how to get out you have first of all to free him from the misleading influence of the question.[30]

The tyranny of this paradigm can be resisted by taking a look at our language. Two typically Wittgensteinian probes would be: Is some object (however fashioned) always correlated with working, meaningful language? Need it be?[31] Wittgenstein consistently found that the answer to these questions was negative, and that putting them generated a healthy respect for language-games and grammar. We have already seen the results of these questions in our discussion of conceptual borders and what Tracy calls "meaning." The issues of "meaningfulness" and "truth" are no less confused.

Tracy's picture for meaningfulness is the basic and controlling insight of <u>Blessed Rage for Order</u>. It is an a priori conviction that language functions as a re-presentation. It claims to be verified in the discovery and disclosure of the very experience it posits. Theology can be public because it appeals to the public experience of basic faith. A phenomenological moment is therefore required to disclose meaningfulness.

> Throughout, we shall employ the word "meaningful" to refer to that intrinsic relationship between a mediating symbol, image, metaphor, myth or concept and the immediate lived experience of the self.[32]

This picture of language leads Tracy to speak of the expressions of this "originating lived experience" as "derivative."[33] The role of language is being overlooked.

The lines of our Wittgensteinian critique of Tracy's theory are by now clear. There is a failure to attend to one's language. This failure is linked to the conviction that language is merely a vehicle for experience. Experience becomes the criterion for what Tracy calls "meaningfulness" and "truth."

Many points from our earlier discussions of Ludwig Wittgenstein come to mind in the course of this discussion of David Tracy. One might think of "game," for instance, when reading Tracy on "religious" or "basic faith." One might be more careful about too strict an appeal to experience, if he had the example of "tove" before his eyes. But, whether or not these particular remarks are useful in looking at Tracy's particular theory, their point remains relevant: in philosophical investigations one must continually recall the home of a word and attend to use and usage. The remark on "imagination" comes to mind.

> One ought to ask, not what images are or what happens when one imagines anything, but how the word "imagination" is used. But that does not mean that I want to talk only about words. For the question as to the nature of the imagination is as much about the word "imagination" as my question is. And I am only saying that this question is not to be decided--neither for the person who does the imagining, nor for anyone else--by pointing; nor yet

129

by a description of any process. The first question also asks for a word to be explained; but it makes us expect a wrong kind of answer.[34]

This is good advice for David Tracy, since he too is set off in the wrong direction by a false question. A fascination with a picture of how language must mean creates a radical inattention to the actual context of use and usage. One begins to think that clarity is to be found by focusing more and more closely on the relevant experience. "Here it is easy to get into that dead-end in philosophy, where one believes that the difficulty of the task consists in our having to describe phenomena that are hard to get hold of, the present experience that slips quickly by, or something of the kind."[35] The difficulty, of course, remains conceptual.

Wittgenstein admonishes us to look at the game words play and to be aware of grammatical influence. These imperatives do have consequences for a project like Tracy's. No fixed, final, a-historical border for concepts like "religious" appears. Even if it did, simply linking a concept with a referent would not grant meaning. Words mean within an ongoing weave of life and language. To remove them from this flow is an invitation to misunderstanding. Reliance upon the theory that meaning is a correlation of words, thoughts, and the world will not bring the inquirer to clarity. For at the very point when clarity demands that one watch the game being played and recall the grammar at work, she is riveted to the object, the image, the experience. The picture of meaning as a function of re-presentation is counter-productive and insufficient.

There are no absolutely circumscribed concepts to mesh perfectly with discrete facts. The requirement for a pin-point scientific definition of terms is not met by our ordinary language. A single word frequently evidences various behaviors. A pond is deep, but so are Wittgenstein's writings and student's papers. The sky is blue, as is my desk blotter. Yet I may be blue as well. Uses fluctuate.

> We are unable clearly to circumscribe the concepts we use; not because we don't know their real definition, but because there is no real "definition" to them. To suppose that there must be would be like supposing that whenever children play with a ball they play a game according to strict rules.[36]

The borders of our concepts are just not that exact _in se_, though they are quite precise in context.

Proper nouns are no better off. For example, one may debate about Moses and never depend upon a rigid permanent boundary or a precise correlation.

Consider this example. If one says "Moses did not exist," this may mean several things. It may mean:

the Isrealites did not have a <u>single</u> leader when they withdrew from Egypt--or: their leader was not called Moses--or: there cannot have been anyone who accomplished all that the Bible relates of Moses--or: etc., etc.³⁷

Which description of Moses is essential? How do you know? "By 'Moses' I understand the man who did what the Bible relates of Moses, or at any rate a good deal of it." How much? Which things can be sacrificed? "Has the name 'Moses' got a fixed and unequivocal use for me in all possible cases?"³⁸ Not really. But it has a clear referent! We cannot say a priori, prescinding from application, what always and in every use must be a defining characteristic of "Moses." Rather, what is essential is a function of the circumstances.³⁹ Depending on a referent to provide the controlling boundary is misleading. Meaning is not always and everywhere a function of a definite referential arrangement and rules for use are not absolute, but contextual. There are various uses in various language-games. And, of course, we have not even got a referent outside of the language-game.

Any version of the name-object model for meaning will have other serious flaws at well. For meaning is certainly not a function of linking a word with objects--whether it is the "simple objects" of the <u>Tractatus</u> or common gross objects such as a tress, or vague objects such as basic faith. The meaning of a name is not given by its referent.

Let us first discuss <u>this</u> point of the argument: that a word has no meaning if nothing corresponds to it. It is important to note that the word "meaning" is being used illicitly if it is used to signify the thing that "corresponds" to the word. That is to confound the meaning of a name with the <u>bearer</u> of the name. When Mr. N. N. dies one says that the bearer of the name dies, not that the meaning dies. And it would be nonsensical to say that, for if the name ceased to have meaning it would make no sense to say "Mr. N. N. is dead."⁴⁰

We often have meaning without being able to find any correspondence. The color red may disappear and yet "red" maintains meaningfulness. One cannot claim, in that case, that memory provides a sort of indestructible referent for the word. This is to presume that we always remember it right. But what is the criterion for remembering it <u>right</u>? We just do not use memory to settle such disagreements.⁴¹ Meaning is not baldly donated or retracted by any thing or by any memory of a thing. The search for meaningfulness must move from the realm of metaphysics to use in a language-game. If speaking of "red" (or "religious") does cease to make sense, it will be because a paradigm of usage has dropped out of our language and not because "red" has lost a referent.⁴²

If meaning is a function of re-presentation, how are the presentation and the presented joined? How does it all work? By thought? By intention? How do you know this word will hook up with that experience? Tracy is vague on this. Wittgenstein is not. The critique of ostensive definition may cause the theorist to fall back on "that gaseous medium," the mind. The alignment of the linguistic picture is accomplished by a mental process. A hidden activity supplies--in ways unknown--the exact linking of the parallel structures of meaningfulness. "The signs of our language seem dead without those mental processes."[43] The mind becomes a philosophical <u>deus ex machina</u>: it is cranked out to fill in the gaps in the theory's plot. It miraculously insures that the proper experience is linked with the proper word.

> Thought can as it were <u>fly</u>, it doesn't have to walk. You do not understand your own transactions, that is to say you do not have a synoptic view of them, and you as it were project your lack of understanding into the idea of a medium in which the most astounding things are possible.[44]

But from Wittgenstein's perspective, ostensive definition--mental or digital--is inconclusive and secondary. Mental pointing and thought do not ground language but are grounded by language. It is ignorance of use and language-games which generates the need to posit mental projection. Typically, Wittgenstein finds that what gives life to signs is not any mysterious process in the mind but our language. "Every sign by <u>itself</u> seems dead. <u>What</u> gives it life?--in use it is alive."[45]

The other foundational issue in theology is that of truth. The same confusing and captivating picture is in control. The basic standard is that of adequacy of representation. The task of philosophical reflection is disclosure. Just as phenomenology is invoked to disclose the meaning and meaningfulness of experience and language, so metaphysics is needed to "disclose the true conditions of the possibility of that experience."[46]

> Religion, in short, is basically a representative phenomenon whose cognitive claims can be investigated only by a mode of reflection (metaphysics) whose task is precisely the investigation of all claims to re-present our basic beliefs and the conditions of the possibility of all our existing and understanding.[47]

It does seem that the problem of truth and the solution of metaphysical inference are being adjusted by definition to fit certain a priori requirements. Why is it that cognitive claims can be investigated <u>only</u> by a metaphysics? Why is it that only a certain type of metaphysics seems to fill the bill? The definition of the metaphysical task and the definition of the nature of a cognitive claim are functions of Tracy's prior definition of meaning and language. Unnoted definitions are directing inquiry again;

the representative paradigm and its final appeal to experience are clearly in evidence.

Tracy contends that it can be shown that "God" designates what it is about our experience of the whole that justifies our faith, what makes it "on the mark" and true. He claims that to deny "God" as the referent would be self-contradictory for "any intelligent and rational ('reflective') inquirer."[48] It would be either a denial of our actual and ineluctable experience or a refusal to make the intelligent inference from it.

> More exactly, only the reality of God, itself reinterpreted in process metaphysical categories, can account for that original and eluctable confidence in the worthwhileness of existence which the ealier analyses of the religious dimensions of our common experience portrayed.[49]

Truth, then, is a matter of correspondence with a referent. Metaphysics draws these lines of correspondence. "The truth claims of such language will need the explicit raising of the question of God as the objective reality for such experiences."[50] One is compelled to notice the apparently unnoticed definitions moving the argument. In the background is a particular picture of how the word "truth" must mean. According to whom is the matter of truth settled by "an objective referent?" Must the question of God be raised in order to address the question of truth? Why? Is this so in non-theistic religious discourse? Is Tracy doing more than redefining "God" in terms of an experience he feels is "ineluctable" and then claiming to discover this God by inference? What is happening to our language here? Factual leaps are being made under verbal cover.

Metaphysics is defined as the investigation of claims to represent basic faith. The question of re-presentation turns out to be the question of the conditions for the possibility of the experience, which turns out to be the question of a coherent and existentially adequate conception of the source for the claimed limit experience and limit language. "Does theistic language adequately re-present the most basic faith presupposed by all existing and understanding? Properly understood, that _is_ the philosophical question of God."[51] Can this concept be shown to be necessarily implied by all of human experiencing and understanding? There are two moves in Tracy's discussion of verification: what referent is implied by the experience? Does a particular conception (theism, Christology) capture the originating experience and its expression? The role of language is again being overlooked. Tracy says rather bluntly, "And yet, the ultimate appeal in both metaphysical and matter-of-fact questions is to experience."[52]

What can this mean? The problem with Tracy's use of the word "true" is the same problem he had with the use of the words "meaning" and "meaningful." An extensive discussion is not needed. At this point, it is enough to point out the value of attention to language. If we take a wider look around, we see that just as meaning is not a function of a parallelism of words, thoughts, and the world, so truth is not simply a correspondence. There is more to it.

> Well, if everything speaks for a hypothesis and nothing against it—is it then certainly true? One may describe it as such. But does it certainly agree with reality, with the facts? With this question you are already going around in a circle.[53]

You are putting questions which set you off in the wrong direction; they turn your gaze away from language. Attempts to skirt the role of language and to go "to the source" are fatal to the search for clarity. Tracy is not attending to his language and consequently he is confusing the facts he wishes to assert with his grammatical definitions. There is a failure to note that what counts as "mirroring reality" or as an "objective referent in the world" may differ from one language-game to another. "How do I know that this colour is red? It would be an answer to say: 'I have learnt English.'"[54]

When do we say that a statement, assertion or proposition is true? It is not when we are overwhelmed by the impact of corresponding objects in the world. These may be a part of the weave, but only a part. There is more at work. A foundation has already been laid.

> The reason why the use of the expression "true or false" has something misleading about it is that it is like saying "it tallies with the facts or it doesn't," and the very thing that is in question is what "tallying" is here.[55]

Whether a face is in grief is determined by the concept of emotion and of this emotion. It is not the result of just looking at "the reality."[56] "We don't understand Chinese gestures any more than Chinese sentences."[57]

Truth is a correspondence, but it is the correspondence of the linguistic life of the community, of the natural history of a word, with the present particular case. It is a correspondence of the ordinary use and context with <u>this</u> particular use and context. It is not a question of the correspondence of objects and words, but of usage and use.[58] So, for example, the statement "It is raining" is true if I know the common usage and apply it in the appropriate situations. If I change either of these conditions, it may be false. Drops of water are falling from the clouds, near me, and so on. This is what we commonly call raining. The statement is true. I do not really understand English that well if I am unsure. Or perhaps I understand the language very well, but fail to notice that the deluge is from my garden sprinkler. The statement may be false. The question of verification—is it raining or not—is first a grammatical one. It is only when usage[59] and use join hands that we begin to speak about what is or is not true. For "verification," "referent," "fact," and "true" are words in a language-game and part of a form of life. "Asking whether and how a proposition can be verified is only a particular way of asking 'How d'you mean.' The answer is a contribution to the grammar of the proposition."[60]

For Tracy, the search for meaningfulness and truth is a search for certain experiences. This selective focus blurs the linguistic surroundings. At work quietly are a captivating picture and a host of special definitions. Within this private system, he may have his meaningfulness and his truth. But it is a rather uninteresting manipulation which can claim to move little else. The results are conceptually and factually confusing. Overlooking language is not the way to conduct interesting and fruitful investigations. It is not the way to public clarity in theological discourse. Tracy's general commitment to a revisionist theology is a move in the right direction, but its successful realization requires a slightly larger map and a linguistic orientation.

Wittgenstein and Foundations

Tracy's attachment to the picture of language as a representation of the basic faith experience is not stupid. The failure to look at language and the compulsion to think how it must work instead is a persistent danger in philosophical and theological inquiry. It certainly was for Wittgenstein. Furthermore, the appeal to experience is an attempt to produce a theology that is public. A discourse over matters religious that is guided by public criteria, warrants, and arguments would be useful in our pluralistic and secular culture. Tracy's false step is seeing the problem as existential and cognitional and the solution as a disclosure of suitable experience. The borders of meaning and meaningfulness become an obvious question of the experience liberated by phenomenology. The question of truth is a logical inference to the roots of that experience as charted by a metaphysics. Public foundations are displayed by mediating certain basic experiences "by our own powers of intelligent and critical introspection."[61] The picture at work is one of a parallelism which gives rise to meaning and meaningfulness, and a correspondence which establishes truth.

The basic error is using words but overlooking words, not seeing the fundamental function of words but looking instead for the supposedly deeper object level to which they point. While Tracy is concerned with meaning and truth as foundational, he overlooks the linguistic roots of these and devotes most of his effort to a search for elements and relations that can be plugged into the already presumed parallelism of words and objects. Tracy's method advances language as central and yet refuses to take language seriously on its own terms. He does not take a look. Words cause our difficulties and their uses are what we must describe. But these are not introspectible items. ". . .it shows a fundamental misunderstanding, if I am inclined to study the headache I have now in order to get clear about the philosophical problem of sensation."[62] There is a need for linguistic conversion. This will cure

Tracy's confusion. Since the problems with which he is concerned are conceptual and not scientific, "We must do away with all explanation, and description alone must take its place."[63]

The meaning of a word is discovered by looking at its use in a language. And use is not a discrete object or a sophisticated surrogate for an object. It is a complex of gestures, thoughts, feelings, actions and so forth. This is true not just of words like "apple" but also of words like "thought." Words designate no single item--inside or outside of the mind. Rather, they describe a pattern which recurs, with different variations, in the weave of our life.[64] A good way to see this is to ask, how did I learn (or teach) this word? How would I teach a child the word "toothache?" Suddenly one sees that what is needed first is not an object or an experience, but a whole context, a form of life.

"Why can't a dog simulate pain? Is he too honest?"[65] We laugh because dogs just are not human enough to pretend--or to be honest. They do not share a form of life which makes this a real possibility. The word is not used in that way. Think of cartoon chairs or pink panthers that talk: they are believable because they are given as many human attributes as possible. The more the lion is "one of us" the more likely it is that he just might talk. The meaning of a word ("talk," "feel," "religious") is a complex of usage and use in the weave of life. Much more is at work than the simple apprehension of a simple experience. That is why we want to look to use and not just to a referent. To call for attention to use is not to advance a theory. It is not to make use a new object of correlation. It is not a denial of pain, thought, grief, or other experiences. It is a turn to language. It is a call for clarity on what the use is here. Once the use is clear, one has the meaning. Quibbles about what sort of object might grant meaning disappear.

The trouble with David Tracy's filling of his revisionist prescription is not that he talks about experience, but that he does so without also attending to his language. Certain experiences may very well be part of the use of a word. This is different than saying or presuming that experience is an identifiable, recurring element which insures meaning. A good deal of stage-setting has already been done by the time one is ready to discuss the presence or absence of an experience as part of the meaning or truth of a word.[66] When one pronounces some object as the clear giver of life to mere words, a weave of life and language is read into the situation and not noted. A major error made is that the inquirer overlooks language precisely because it is doing its job. A whole form of life is projected into the object or experience and its unnoticed presence makes it look as if the object or experience were doing all the work. "Human beings are entangled in the net of language and do not know it."[67] And there is no getting under the net. This is where Tracy's project goes astray. What he ends up with is a confusion of terms, of the factual and the grammatical, the presumption of a particular model for how all language works, and a predictable lack of clarity.

The search for foundations is undertaken to bring clarity and understanding but it often brings a thick and impenetrable fog. Wittgenstein reorients us and disperses the mists. There is something overlooked by foundationalism: language. There is a presumption that constructing a metaphysics or an epistemology--a foundation--is the best guarantee of a philosophical or theological position. Wittgenstein denies the value and radicality of any such move. Instead he invites us to a new linguistic self-consciousness. The justification for our language is not simply a matter of accurate mirroring or anchoring in a privileged representation. In fact the various moves in an investigation (e.g., doubt, certainty, mistakes, justifications) have their meaning only in a language. Epistemology and ontology are not necessarily justification. Justification is a function of words and sentences in context, an operation within a practical form of life. What is at stake is not a theory but a way of living and speaking.

A justification is whatever we appropriately call a justification. It is not a matter of causes explained or objects found but of use in a language-game. Who will deny that justification is a word and means what we say it means in our language? Justification is not a brick. The whole business sounds rather banal. An obvious fact has simply been noted. But it is a fact commonly ignored and resisted. No complex theory here, no counter-position, no foundation; just a reminder that language plays a role. It is this simple move which the foundationalist finds so difficult to appreciate.

Justification does come to an end, but it does not end in a foundation.

> If I have exhausted the justifications I have reached bedrock, and my spade is turned. Then I am inclined to say: "This is simply what I want to do."[68]

Such remarks often leave critics aghast: Is this not relativism? But this worry springs more from an attachment to foundationalism than from an understanding of Wittgenstein. Relativism is a term of opprobrium used to condemn a competing view of the foundations for true knowing. Wittgenstein eschews the competition. He does not offer a better view of the connection between word and world, a sharper representation. He merely points out the power of language and warns us to be self-conscious and respectful. "'So you are saying that human agreement decides what is true and what is false?'" No. The Wittgensteinian therapist is redirecting the query.

> It is what human beings say that is _true_ and false; and they agree in the _language_ they use. That is not agreement in opinions but in forms of life.[69]

Justification is first a social transaction and not a link between a knowing subject and a known object. It does not constitute reality, but it does tell us what counts as reality, what counts as a judgment of truth, and so forth. Meaning and truth, then, depend upon agreement in human language and not on some form of representation. It is only within a context of usage and use that we tag something as "true" or "false."

This does not mean that anything goes. When your spade is turned, you must admit that this is simply what you do. But that does not mean that use and usage are whimsical. It does mean that security is no longer a function of finding a correspondence with "the nature of things." "What stands fast does so, not because it is intrinsically obvious or convincing; it is rather held fast by what lies around it."[70] Wittgenstein wants us to take a wider look around. Grammatical rules are arbitrary in that they give no extra-linguistic justification. But there are still standards for going on correctly, truly, and meaningfully. "Grammatical rules are arbitrary, but their application is not."[71] The fact that there are no compelling foundations does not mean that there are no rules. And the fact that there are rules does not mean that there must be foundations.

Raising the question of relativism as a critique of Wittgenstein or of Wittgenstein's usefulness is less a point of dialectic than an attempt to maneuver him into the foundationalist framework he seeks to avoid. Since the Wittgensteinian shift is radically non-theoretical and non-foundational, it has no position on the theory concerning the relativity of foundations. Asking someone to turn from a fixation on mirroring, asking them to leave the search for foundations, does not locate one as a relativist or a non-relativist. That quest is abandoned. Attention is turned to another question: What in fact do you mean by relativism and how so? Attention is turned to language.

A related and equally misplaced debate has arisen over so-called Wittgensteinian fideism.[72] Does not Wittgenstein divide language into separate and autonomous compartments, into forms of life and language-games? Does this not lead to the groundless loyalty of a fideism? Are various realms of discourse not thereby insulated from any serious critique? Can, for example, those who do not accept the religious language-game raise any criticisms of religion? The isolated games supposedly posited by Ludwig Wittgenstein seem to allow no possibility of a conversation which crosses games or forms of life. This means that disagreements cannot be resolved. Disputants can only continue to insist on their positions. There is no language in which those who operate from differing games can formulate mutually understandable arguments. Each game or form of life is shut off from the other and is sovereign within its own kingdom. Discourse is not public. These are some of the notes of what has been called Wittgensteinian fideism. From a Wittgensteinian point of view, this fideism is a web of confusions.

Much of the literature on Wittgensteinian fideism is generated by a false understanding of Wittgenstein's later work and an irrepressible fascination with foundations. There may well be fideists who clothe themselves in Wittgensteinian garb. Certainly religious or philosophical fideists can frame their positions in Wittgensteinian jargon. Yet Wittgenstein's own work is directed elsewhere. He asks about the role of language in particular philosophical discussions. His approach is radically non-foundational and non-systematic. He does not draw absolute or universal boundaries to language-games, nor does he suggest that language be viewed as a mosaic of tight linguistic nuclei. In fact, such positions are the target of his critique.

There is no definite theory of the language-game (or form of life) and so there are no fideist implications of the theory. Wittgenstein does not advance terms such as "forms of life" or "language-game" as strictly defined or consistent factors in a system. As theories, these notions are notoriously ill-defined and vague. They are useful and clear in their few particular applications. Wittgenstein uses the concept of a language-game as a dispensable tool to turn attention to language, and not a permanent gear in a great machine. The shape of this tool is not indelibly fixed but is a function of its use. It shows a fundamental misreading of Wittgenstein's later work to ask, what is the definition of a "language-game" or what are its theoretical implications? It is more fruitful to ask why Wittgenstein uses the concept here and how it brings a reader to a new perspective. A universal definition would solve nothing in philosophy, it would loosen no knots. And so the Wittgensteinian shift is not merely a trendy attempt to replace epistemology with a philosophy of language. It is not a shift in techniques for plying the same old search for foundations. Yet those in search of foundations cannot resist mixing Wittgenstein's ad hoc specifics into a panacea.

What is Wittgenstein offering us? Wittgenstein's investigations offer no foundation either for philosophy or for theology, but they do offer clarity and the possibility of conversation. They offer no theory, but they do offer a therapy. Working through Wittgenstein's <u>Philosophical Investigations</u> is an activity caculated to help us habituate ourselves to the wider linguistic context. The goal is to clear up muddles. It is language which proves to be crucial and not any theory--even a theory about language.

You cannot get under the net of language to a foundation; you cannot go further back. To say that my spade is turned is not to say that I have hit a foundation but merely to say that digging is at an end. This is not an appeal to some "already-out-there-now-real" or "in-here-real." Rather it is an appeal to the social, the intersubjective, the linguistic. The certainty afforded by an ontological edifice is a reflection of its acceptance by the community of discourse. It does not merely reflect confrontation with compelling objects or experiences. "What looks as if it had to exist, is part of the language."[75] But Wittgenstein's interest in depth grammar should not be construed as an attempt to discover <u>the</u> logic of our language or to establish linguistic foundations. There are only the shifting sands of language, the ebb and flow of ordinary usage and use. Neither the examples studied nor the tools taken up are foundational.

Illusory "houses of cards" are felled.[74] Wittgenstein wants to give us a perspective in which the linguistic horizon is clear and obvious. The goal is not a complete "natural history" of all our words. Linguistic awareness cannot be nailed down once and for all in a "Wittgensteinian" epistemology, a "Wittgensteinian" philosophy of language, or a "Wittgensteinian" edition of the Oxford English Dictionary. It is an activity and a perspective. Any search for a pre-linguistic or non-linguistic starting point will be frustrating and futile. What we need is a method, a method which creates the habit of looking in the right direction.

Wittgenstein's remarks are tools for the appropriation of this new type of methodological self-consciousness. If it happens that one or the other of them is not useful at a particular time, then one simply drops it back into the toolbox. Method is ad hoc practice, not a system.[75] A Wittgensteinian is not only someone who attends to cases, but someone who attends to cases in such a way that she becomes linguistically, empirically, and methodologically self-conscious. This is the grammatical method of the later Wittgenstein. We are not dazzled by new knowledge brought forth; we are amazed by reminders of what we already know. From this new perspective, some philosophical puzzles may dissolve. Looking at the grammar involved in important issues may jar readers into taking a new and wider look around.[76] This is a fruitful result. There are no final positions or philosophical dogmas. There are no doctrines to which one must assent, no new theories. There is a new method. G. E. Moore sums it up well in his notes on Wittgenstein's lectures in 1930-1931:

> He went on to say that, though philosophy has now been 'reduced to a matter of skill,' yet this skill, like other skills, is very difficult to acquire. One difficulty was that it required a 'sort of thinking' to which we are not accustomed and to which we have not been trained—a sort of thinking very different from what is required in the sciences. And he said that the required skill could not be acquired merely by hearing lectures: discussion was essential. As regards his own work, he said it did not matter whether his results were true or not; what mattered was that 'a method had been found.'[77]

In order to read Wittgenstein one must understand that for him "the search says more than the discovery."[78] By bumping our heads against the limits of language we bring into view the linguistic spectacles through which we construe the world. For this reason, "in philosophizing we may not terminate a disease of thought. It must run its natural course, and slow cure is all important."[79] A skill is being developed. The Philosophical Investigations is a workbook, a philosophical therapy. Its fullest contribution lies not in what it says to us, but in what it does to us.

The work of the later Wittgenstein is a personal invitation to a personal dialogue and a personal investigation. To understand the Philosophical Investigations is to read it as a work of confession and persuasion. Throughout it Wittgenstein discovers confusion in his own thinking and works through it by looking at language. Like all good confessions it invites us to join in self-scrutiny. And confession is a means to persuasion. By confessing linguistic confusion in particular cases attention is turned to the actual grammar at work. The real ground comes into view. He wants us to acquire the skill of clearing up our own muddles.

> In giving all these examples I am not aiming at some kind of completeness, some classification of psychological concepts. They are only meant to enable the reader to shift for himself when he encounters conceptual difficulties.[80]

In the linguistic therapy of Wittgenstein the focus is on our own language, our own experience of confusion, our own recollection of use, and our own appropriation of a new methodological praxis, of a pervasive linguistic awareness. The consequent loosening of certain philosophical knots is found to be most persuasive and habit forming.

The simplicity of Wittgenstein's remedy for philosophical complexities and his failure to be foundational generate a certain resistance to his work. When he is taken seriously, he may be misinterpreted as a philosopher of language, or a lexicographer, or taken as a petty schoolmaster clucking over the grammatical misdeeds of others. But Wittgenstein does not wish to proscribe or prescribe use. He wants to note use. Wittgenstein is not interested in preventing various misuses of words. He is hopelessly addicted to description and differences. He wants to describe how particular words are being used. Our problems are not caused by our failure to obey the rules of language, but by our failure to notice what we are doing with our language. This marks a difference between his perspective and the theories of more ordinary linguistic philosophers. It is not a minor difference.

For Wittgenstein, taking a descriptive attitude, really looking at concrete uses, is a key move. When we do look instead of thinking, we see many games and grammars and become more aware of language at work. This provides not a muzzle but a release. "Don't _for heaven's sake_, be afraid of talking nonsense! But you must pay attention to your nonsense."[81] The earlier Wittgenstein told us what we could not say, the later Wittgenstein simply wants us to pay attention to what we do say.

> Should it be said that I am using a word whose meaning I don't know, and so I am talking nonsense? Say what you choose, so long as it does

> not prevent you from seeing the facts about the use of the words. (And when you see them there is a good deal that you will not say.)[82]

David Tracy's revisionist project is a case in point. A <u>Wittgensteinian</u> revisionism might look quite different. When concrete grammatical practice is looked at, many a striking theory may appear bland. A Wittgensteinian would not bar someone like Tracy from going where he wills with his words, but he can wonder if the trip will be exciting. There might be a good deal that a Wittgensteinian revisionist would not say, and a good deal more that might get done.

In our search for clear and fruitful conversation on important issues, we think that the solution to our confusion must be a critical foundation, a privileged representation, or an experience. While we search for these, we overlook a solution. There must be more to it than looking at language and describing use. After all, we are talking about what makes things true or false or meaningful on the most basic level. For this reason, we seek an explanation in metaphysics, epistemology, or philosophy of language. On Wittgenstein's advice, what we really need is description of our language at work.

> Here we come up against a remarkable and characteristic phenomenon in philosophical investigation: the difficulty--I might say--is not that of finding the solution but rather that of recognizing as the solution something that looks as if it were only preliminary to it. This is connected, I believe, with our wrongly expecting an explanation, whereas the solution of the difficulty is a description, if we give it the right place in our considerations. If we dwell upon it, and do not try to get beyond it. The difficulty here is: to stop.[83]

It is difficult to stop. It is difficult to recognize that we are at bottom when we still feel like digging. What we need is not a theoretical foundation for inquiry but a linguistic sensitivity of the sort advocated by the later Wittgenstein. The shift called for is very different and very plain. But looking at the linguistic glasses on your nose does work. Muddles are cleared up. Puzzles dissolve before our eyes. Confusions are noted. Certain uses show themselves to be mere ornaments while conversation about the issues is more pointed and durable.

> A person with "common sense" who reads one of the earlier philosophers, thinks (and not without justification): "Sheer nonsense!" When he hears me, he thinks: "Just insipid commonplaces!" Again, with justification. And thus, the look of philosophy has changed.[84]

What sounds so bland as a thesis has profound results as a praxis.

As we have seen, this methodological shift has serious implications for doing theology. Attention to one's own use of words in theologizing may result in abandoning a whole mode of thinking. There is no Wittgensteinian theology, but theology can be done from a Wittgensteinian perspective. While there is a place for the consideration of religious issues and dilemmas, there is no place for sweeping claims, theses, foundations and the like. A good deal in theology may be said differently.

It is possible, for example, to revise David Tracy's revisionism. The problematic as set by Tracy may be affirmed, while his actual solution is found wanting. It is not that Tracy's epistemology is wrong, but that epistemology is not the solution to his troubles. It leads to overlooking language and the confusion of substantive and verbal problems. Tracy is concerned that theology be public discourse, yet he generates a theology rife with private definitions and unnoted linguistic manipulations. He insists on an appeal to empirically available data and the centrality of the issues of meaning and truth. Yet the actual use and usage of his words fades before a priori demands that language be representative and limited. Does Tracy look for accuracy of representation when he might better look at the game being played? Tracy is committed to method as the way out of the quandries of pluralism and secularism. He is convinced that the linking of language and method is the key, but is driven to forge a theory. He looks for a phenomenology and a metaphysic that thematize experience appropriately and adequately. Matthew Lamb's rejection of this theoretical solution to the problem of method is correct. Tracy does not need a better theory; he needs a better way of going on. Wittgenstein would suggest the usefulness of a self-conscious attention to usage and use. David Tracy's attention is on experience, not on language. His investigations attempt to be factual precisely where they should strive to be grammatical or conceptual.

Contemporary theological inquiry would do well to affirm the revisionist openness to critique and dedication to a public, methodologically self-conscious, and linguistic theology. While Tracy's search for priviledged foundations is a misplaced effort, his search for clarity in theological investigations is not. The revisionist framework might be stated as a series of imperatives: be publicly accountable, be open to revision, be faithful to both common human experience and the Christian tradition as theological sources, be attentive to the criteria for meaning and truth in thinking theologically. Wittgenstein would add one more imperative: Look at the language-games played and notice the natural (ordinary) home of the words you use. A good deal in theology might then be said differently. Or not at all.

How might a Wittgensteinian revisionism look? It would be, most of all, an attempt to keep conversation on religious matters alive. Inattention to language can tangle investigations and garble communications. Tracy is very clear that the reason he is interested in fundamental theology is to preserve and promote genuine conversation. He insists that theology must be public discourse. For Wittgenstein, conversation means an end to the search for foundations and the development of a linguistic tropism. The fundamental move in theology—as in philosophy—is conversion to grammatical awareness. It is not the construction of "objective" or "cognitive" foundations, but a shift to a new horizon for looking at puzzles. "Work in philosophy—as in architecture—is in reality rather work on oneself, on one's own outlook. On one's way of seeing things."[85] We do not need a set of permanent limits or rules. We do need to know where we are, but for this it is enough to put out a few temporary markers for a particular case. The point is not to acquire new information but to assemble those reminders which will bring before us what we already know. This brings clarity to our inquiry.

Neither theology nor philosophy is about words. A Wittgensteinian revisionist theologian will strive to meet the exigences of modern reflection on religion. Theology must proceed in a manner that is genuinely public and a genuine discourse. One cannot afford to unwittingly speak only her own language or to ignore the variations in the languages of others. By abstracting from actual linguistic commerce, theologians place themselves at the mercy of simplistic parallels and the misleading analogies of surface grammar. They invite unintelligibility into their investigations. Language should not be a block to inquiry. When philosophers and theologians are merely fighting over words, conversation is at a standstill.

It is for this reason that this present book on Wittgenstein and theology does not end with an outline of "the new theology." There are no Wittgensteinian theological doctrines. From God and religion to sexual ethics, issues come into a different light when their grammatical unconscious is probed. But the Wittgensteinian shift is methodic, linguistic, perspectival, and personal. It does not dictate constructive positions, it keeps the discussion going. A Wittgensteinian theology will strive for clarity in discussion by looking to language and by being sensitive to its games and to the role of grammar. The preceding pages have attempted to demonstrate the nature and possibility of a new theological dialogue with Ludwig Wittgenstein. Learning from Witgenstein could mean the end of many theological confusions and the stimulation of conversation on some of the most intriguing human concerns. But if Ludwig Wittgenstein does come to have an impact on theological ruminations, it will not be because his theory is correct, but because his praxis is helpful.

Notes

1. OC, 471.

2. Ricoeur discusses the hermeneutics of recollection and suspicion in the first three chapters of his Freud and Philosophy: An Essay on Interpretation, trans. Denis Savage (New Haven: Yale University Press, 1970), especially pp. 23-36.

3. These views are not peculiar to Tracy, but rather are adopted and integrated by him from the work of Paul Ricoeur and Schubert Ogden. The actual charting of the genetic and eclectic relationship between Tracy and his sources cannot be taken up here. It is sufficient to note that in trying to grasp the nature and direction of Tracy's thought it is often fruitful to refer to Ricoeur's picture of the relationship of thought, language, and faith and to Ogden's compatible process version of foundational human experience. Tracy's integration of Lonergan with these other points of view is nowhere critically grounded. Consequently, while he might seek to escape a Wittgensteinian critique by appeal to Lonergan's method, it remains that he does not actually employ that perspective as foundational.

4. BRO, p. 43.

5. PI, 128. "What we are supplying are really remarks on the natural history of human beings; we are not contributing curiosities however, but observations which no one has doubted, but which have escaped remark only because they are always before our eyes." PI, 415.

6. PI, 133.

7. BRO, p. 69.

8. BRO, p. 71 and p. 118, n. 92.

9. PI, 47.

10. The implications here have broad import. For example, recent research suggests that scientists who claim to have taught human language to animals may have skewed their experiments by unconscious projection and cueing. See Herbert S. Terrace, Nim: A Chimpanzee Who Learned Sign Language (New York: Alfred A. Knopf, 1980) and Thomas A. Sebeok and Donna Jean Umiker-Sebeok, eds., Speaking of Apes: A Critical Anthology of Two-Way Communication With Man (New York: Plenum Publishing Corp., 1980).

11. BRO, p. 14.

12. BRO, p. 8.

13. BRO, pp. 154-55.

14. Ernest Becker, The Denial of Death (New York: Free Press, 1973).

15. RC, II, 3.

16. Van A. Harvey, "The Pathos of Liberal Theology," Journal of Religion 56 (October, 1976) 389. This type of thinking does persist in Analogical, though veiled by the introduction of the word "uncanny." See pp. 164, 339ff.

17. PI 128. The slippery nature of theoretical explanation is well presented in an old New Yorker cartoon by Stan Hunt. A professor holding forth at a cocktail party remarks: "In theory, yes, Mrs. Wilkins. But also, in theory, no."

18. BRO, p. 205.

19. BRO, p. 215.

20. BRO, p. 10.

21. Philosophy and theology are not sciences, they do not have the long tradition of exact and fixed meanings to rely upon. Clarity is important, but the key is not to be scientific. The scientific stream of life and thought is very different from the philosophical.

22. PI, 116.

23. PI, 116.

24. BRO, p. 69.

25. BRO, pp. 74-76.

26. PI, 49.

27. BRO, p. 34.

28. BRO, p. 14. See also BRO, p. 79: "On the one hand, the meanings discovered as adequate to our common human experience must be compared to the meanings disclosed as appropriate to the Christian tradition in order to discover how similar, different, or identical the former meanings are in relationship to the latter."

29. BB, p. 1.

30. BB, p. 169.

31. Hallett, Definition, pp. 73-75.

32. BRO, 66. Experience is primary. Tracy cites with approval the dictum of Hartshorne: "A thought which does not mean by virtue of an experience is simply a thought which does not mean." Man's Vision of God and the Logic of Theism (Chicago: Willett, Clark, 1941) as quoted in BRO, p. 198, n. 68.

33. BRO, p. 68.

34. PI, 370.

35. PI, 436. The number continues: "Where we find ordinary language too crude, and it looks as if we were having to do, not with phenomena of every-day, but with ones that 'easily elude us, and, in their coming to be and passing away, produce those others as an average effect.' (Augustine: Manifestissima et usitatissima sunt, et eadem rusus nimis latent, et nova est inventio eorum.)"

36. BB, p. 25. BB, p. 27: "Many words in this sense then don't have a strict meaning. But this is not a defect. To think it is would be like saying that the light of my reading lamp is no real light at all because it has no sharp boundary." One is free, of course, to give a word a specially limited sense, as many philosophers and theologians do. But one must not then proceed as if such a concept will ever coincide with the shifting borders of actual usage. See BB, p. 19 and PI, 29, 68, 81.

37. PI, 79.

38. PI, 79.

39. The meaning of a word might change and noting that change might end a puzzle. What if, for example, after a long discussion and disagreement, I suddenly sigh, "Well, he did die around A.D. 1204, didn't he?" Our argument over Moses may dissolve.

40. PI, 40.

41. PI, 56. "To see that this is not necessary remember that I could have given him the order, 'imagine a yellow patch.' Would you still be inclined to assume that he first imagines a yellow patch, just understanding my order, and then imagines a yellow patch to match the first? (Now I don't say this is not possible. Only, putting it in this way immediately shows you that it need not happen. This, by the way, illustrates the method of philosophy.)" BB, p. 12.

42. PI, 57. "For the fact that we cannot conceive of something 'glowing grey' belongs neither to the physics nor to the psychology of colour." RC, I, 40.

43. <u>BB</u>, p. 3. Wittgenstein, of course, is attacking a theory very different from Tracy's. But the attack is still instructive.

44. <u>Z</u>, 273. See also <u>PI</u>, 339. <u>BB</u>, pp. 73-74: "The meaning of the expression depends entirely on how we go on using it. Let's not imagine the meaning as an occult connection the mind makes between a word and a thing, and that this connection <u>contains</u> the whole usage of a word as the seed might be said to contain the tree." <u>BB</u>, p. 42: "The mental act seems to perform in a miraculous way what could not be performed by any act of manipulating symbols. Now when the temptation to think that in some sense the whole calculus must be present at the same time vanishes, there is no more point in <u>postulating</u> the existence of a peculiar kind of mental act alongside of our expression. This, of course, doesn't mean that we have shown that peculiar acts of consciousness do not accompany the expressions of our thoughts! Only we no longer say that they <u>must</u> accompany them." For a fuller sense of this discussion consult <u>PI</u>, 138-242, 316-62 and 428-65.

45. <u>PI</u>, 432; <u>Z</u>, 45.

46. <u>BRO</u>, p. 69.

47. <u>BRO</u>, p. 155.

48. <u>BRO</u>, p. 159.

49. <u>BRO</u>, p. 174.

50. <u>BRO</u>, p. 118, n. 92. See also <u>BRO</u>, p. 183 where Tracy clearly states that "the primary existential use for the word 'God' is to refer to the objective ground in reality itself for those limit-languages and limit-experiences of an ultimate worth of our existence...."

51. <u>BRO</u>, p. 154.

52. <u>BRO</u>, p. 227, n. 30. <u>BRO</u>, p. 71 states that a particular language or experience "is 'true' when transcendental or metaphysical analysis shows its 'adequacy to experience' by explicating how a particular concept (e.g., time, space, self, or God) functions as a fundamental 'belief' or 'condition of possibility' of all our experience."

53. <u>OC</u>, 191.

54. <u>PI</u>, 381.

55. <u>OC</u>, 199. "Really 'the proposition is either true or false' only means that it must be possible to decide for or against it. But this does not say what the ground for such a decision is like." <u>OC</u>, 200.

56. Z, 225.

57. Z, 219.

58. Hallett, Definition, pp. 166-68. Note that this reliance on usage and use need not be conscious; one does not whip out a table and consult it on past usage and conditions for present use. It is a part of the habitual and ongoing weave of language and life.

59. PI, 356: "One is inclined to say: 'Either it is raining, or it isn't--how I know, how the information has reached me, is another matter.' But then let us put the question like this: what do I call 'information that it is raining?' (Or have I only information of this information too?) And what gives this 'information' the character of information about something? Doesn't the form of our expression mislead us here? For isn't it a misleading metaphor to say 'My eyes give me the information that there is a chair over there'?"

60. PI, 353.

61. BRO, p. 66.

62. PI, 314. Of course, introspectible items or neurological events may be connected with "fear," "hope" and so forth. But Wittgenstein is not interested in these scientific aspects of the problem. He is interested in philosophical problems. Cf. Hallett, Companion, pp. 44-48.

63. PI, 109.

64. PI, p.174.

65. PI, 250.

66. This is the point of many of the episodes in the private language section of Philosophical Investigations. Without engaging that discussion here, the following example from PI, 261 might still prove informative and amusing. It is the case of a man who wants to keep a diary of his experience of a particular sensation. Every time he experiences that sensation he enters an "S" in the diary. He contends that the ground for the meaning of "S" is the experience of the sensation. After raising some doubts about how the man can be sure that it is the same sensation, Wittgenstein pushes the position to its bedrock: "What reason have we for calling "S" the sign for a sensation? For 'sensation' is a word of our common language, not of one intelligible to me alone. So the use of this word stands in need of a justification which everybody understands. And it would not help either to say that it need not be a sensation; that when he writes "S" he has something--and that is all that can be said. 'Has' and 'something' also belong to our common language--so in the end when one is doing philosophy one gets to the point where one would like just to emit an inarticulate sound. But such a sound is an

expression only as it occurs in a particular language-game, which should now be described."

67. PG, 462. Attending to the net is the job of many of Wittgenstein's remarks.

68. PI, 217.

69. PI, 241.

70. OC, 144.

71. Lectures: Cambridge, 1930-1932, p. 58.

72. An excellent review and critique of the discussion is Thomas B. Ommen, "Wittgensteinian Fideism and Theology," Horizons 7 (Fall, 1980) 183-204.

73. PI, 50.

74. PI, 118.

75. Overlooking this has often led interpreters to twist Wittgenstein's work into the one thing it is not. A telling remark of Wittgenstein's is recorded by Gasking and Jackson in "Wittgenstein as a Teacher," p. 54: "I used at one time to say that, in order to get clear how a certain sentence is used, it was a good idea to ask oneself the question 'how would one try to verify such an assertion?' But that's just one way among others of getting clear about the use of a word or sentence. For example, another question which is often very useful to ask oneself is 'how is this word learned?' How would one set about teaching a child to use this word? But some people have turned this suggestion about asking for the verification into a dogma--as if I'd been advancing a theory about meaning."

76. Z, 463: "On mathematics: 'Your concept is wrong. However, I cannot illumine the matter by fighting against your words, but only by trying to turn your attention away from certain expressions, illustrations, images, and towards the employment of the words.'"

77. G. E. Moore, "Wittgenstein's Lectures in 1930-1933," Philosophical Papers (London: George Allen & Unwin, 1963) p. 322.

78. Z, 457. Wittgenstein is quoting St. Augustine. See also PI, 119.

79. Z, 382.

80. PI, p. 206. See also PI 133. For more discussion of the twin themes of confession and persuasion, see Fann, Wittgenstein's Conception of Philosophy, pp. 105-11 and the excellent orientation by Stanley Cavell,

"The Availability of Wittgenstein's Later Philosophy," in George Pitcher, ed., Wittgenstein: The Philosophical Investigations (London: Macmillan and Co., 1970): pp. 151-85.

81. Culture and Value, p. 56.

82. PI, 79.

83. Z, 314.

84. Man, 219, 6 as translated in Hallett, Companion, p. 225.

85. Man, 112, 6 as translated in Hallett, Companion, p. 231. For a brief but clear and interesting expansion of this theme see Debra Aidun, "Wittgenstein, Philosophical Method and Aspect-Seeing," Philosophical Investigations 5 (April 1982): 106-15.

INDEX

Basic faith, 28, 34-41, 55n.37, 59n.69, 121-124

Correlation, 29-31, 33, 35, 69, 72-75, 104-106, 134-135

Criteria, 27, 32-34, 43, 49-51, 118-119

Essence, 90-91, 96-98, 104, 106-107, 119, 131, 147n.36

Experience, 37-40, 48, 51, 55n38, 115, 75, 119-123, 126-128, 149n.66

Form of life, 62, 79n.8

Foundational theology, 2-5, 15-18, 19n.2, 21n.11, 50, 64, 76, 79, 144; David Tracy's models, 6-10, 14-15; Matthew Lamb's models, 10-15

Foundations, 13, 16, 34, 51, 64-66, 79n.10, 90-91, 107, 119, 137-144

God, 32, 58n.60, 118, 133

Grammar, 99-102, 107, 123, 130

Lamb, Matthew, 10-15, 143

Language-game, 93-99

Lonergan, Bernard, 1, 13, 20, 145n.3

Method, 4, 13, 16, 25n.40, 32, 63-66, 76, 80, 87-89, 95, 99, 103-108, 119, 135, 139, 144

Meaning, 28, 41, 48, 50, 53n.19, 53n.20, 77, 87, 96, 99, 105-106, 111n.33, 118, 120, 127-132

Metaphysics, 31-33, 47-49, 75, 100-102

Metz, Johann B., 12-13

Ogden, Schubert M., 28, 48, 54n.23, 54n.27, 118, 145n.3

Phenomenology, 30, 33, 49, 53n.19, 80n.12, 113n.58

Picture theory, 70-75, 77, 93, 134-135

Political theology, 12-14

Praxis, 12-13, 25n.36, 142-144

Relativism, 137-139

Religious, limit character of, 40-46, 49, 124-125

Ricoeur, Paul, 44, 117, 145n.3

Theology, 1, 76, 115n.76; see foundational theology

Truth, 47-50, 53n.20, 118, 120, 132-135

Wittgensteinian fideism, 78n.3, 138-139, 150n.72